$crooge
INVESTING

$crooge INVESTING

The Bargain Hunter's Guide to

DISCOUNTS
FREE SERVICES
SPECIAL
PRIVILEGES

and 99 Other Money-Saving Tips

Mark Skousen

Dearborn
Financial Publishing, Inc.

While a great deal of care has been taken to provide accurate and current information, the ideas, suggestions, general principles and conclusions presented in this book are subject to local, state and federal laws and regulations, court cases and any revisions of same. The reader is thus urged to consult legal counsel regarding any points of law—this publication should not be used as a substitute for competent legal advice.

Publisher: Kathleen A. Welton
Associate Editor: Karen A. Christensen
Interior Design: Irving Perkins Associates
Cover Design: The Publishing Services Group

Published by Dearborn Financial Publishing, Inc.

Printed in the United States of America

Library of Congress Cataloging-in-Publication Data

Skousen, Mark.
    Scrooge investing : the bargain hunter's guide to discounts, free services, special privileges and 99 other money-saving tips / Mark Skousen.
      p. cm.
    Includes index.
    ISBN 0-79310-410-6
    1. Investments.   2. Finance, Personal.   3. Saving and thrift.   I. Title.
HG4521.S615   1992
332.024—dc20
                                      91-46570
                                        CIP

To Gary North, my favorite tightwad

Acknowledgments

MANY PEOPLE helped in preparing this book. I would not go so far as to say that "we spared no expense" to get you this information. That would not fit our Scrooge philosophy. But we did contact the most knowledgeable sources, and paid the necessary expenses, to get this information and timely advice.

In many cases, I relied on several of my in-house experts at Phillips Publishing, such as fellow financial newsletter writers Richard Band, editor of *Profitable Investing*, and Pete Dickinson, editor of *The Retirement Letter*. I also want to thank Gary Alexander, my managing editor, for putting his brainy editing and research skills to work.

Most of all, I wish to thank Michael Ketcher, a freelance writer in San Francisco, for doing much of the spade work, checking details, making phone calls and following up on leads. I hesitate to call his freelance work entirely *free*, but I would say that for me it was quite a bargain!

And bargain hunting is what this whole book is all about.

MARK SKOUSEN

Contents

Tables and Figures

Tables

Figures

SCROOGE INVESTING

The Scrooge Philosophy of Investing

Save your money, Nephew! Pennies saved today are dollars in your pocket tomorrow!

—UNCLE SCROOGE MCDUCK

THE SCROOGE philosophy of investing reminds me of the rich man's most famous fictional character: Uncle Scrooge McDuck!

One of my prize possessions in my trophy case at home is a limited-edition artwork entitled *Uncle Scrooge McDuck: His Life and Times*, written by his creator, Carl Barks. It is a beautiful four-color reproduction of Uncle Scrooge's most popular tales between 1952 and 1967.

As part of the purchase, I received a limited-edition color print of *Wanderers of Wonderlands*, a classic drawing of Uncle Scrooge, along with Donald Duck and Huey, Dewey and Louie, examining a new-found treasure of gems. The print is autographed by Barks. (Now in his 90s, he is living in California, no longer an active artist.)

This collector's edition of Barks's renderings brings back a lot of memories. In the 1950s, I grew up on *Uncle Scrooge* comic books. As a child, I was fascinated by Uncle Scrooge and his adventures with his nephews, his ingenuity in discovering new sources of boundless wealth and his ability to thwart the schemes of the thieving Beagle Boys.

3

I have tried to pass along these boyhood memories to my five children. When I first received this book, I broke the plastic seal around it and read each story aloud to five eager listeners. I realize that it's a *no-no* actually to use a collectible. You're supposed to preserve its pristine condition so as to maintain its highest resale value. (I guess I should have hidden it away in a dark safe-deposit box to avoid all human touch.) I suppose it lost some of its collector's value, but the lessons and joy my children have gained from it seem to far outweigh any monetary reward.

After reading each story, I carefully returned the book to the trophy case and warned the children not to take it down on their own. But apparently the temptation was too strong, and I often found the book outside the trophy case. Stern warnings didn't seem to help. They liked the stories too much and just couldn't resist.

The Appeal of Uncle Scrooge

Barks introduced Uncle Scrooge in a Donald Duck comic book story in the late 1940s. Uncle Scrooge soon became Walt Disney's top-selling comic book in the 1950s, ahead of Donald Duck and Mickey Mouse. What made this irascible character so appealing to the American mind? He was based on another popular fictional miser—Ebenezer Scrooge, Charles Dickens's famous character in *A Christmas Carol.*

Yet, despite his extreme stinginess and fanaticism, there was something universal in Uncle Scrooge's character that could appeal to everyone. His zeal for material wealth gave him many virtues: hard work, individualism, ingenuity, integrity, determination, boldness, adventure and a sense of humor. Yes, he was a skinflint who was not responsive to charitable causes, but he was always willing to get others involved in pursuing a dream.

Above all, Uncle Scrooge was not deceptive and dishonest as so many tycoons are currently portrayed on television or in the movies.

Scrooge earned every penny of his hoard honestly. (The real thieves were the Beagle Boys.) In the first all-Scrooge comic in 1952, Scrooge explained how he made his fortune as a gold digger. Barks explained, "I never thought of Scrooge as I would think of some of the millionaires we have around today, who made their money by exploiting other people to a certain extent. I purposely tried to make it look as if Uncle Scrooge made most of his money back in the days when you could go out in the hills and find riches."

Scrooge not only made a fortune, he kept it. Unlike many instant millionaires, who tend to lose it as fast as they make it, Scrooge worked hard to keep every dime. "I froze my fingers to the bone digging nuggets out of the creeks! And I brought a fortune out, instead of spending it in the honky-tonks!"

Uncle Scrooge has also been accused of being a hoarder. I'm sure you remember pictures of Scrooge diving into his money bin of gold and silver coins nearly 100 feet deep. But that's just for show. Scrooge called it his "petty cash" vault. What you don't see is his real fortune—the oil wells, railroads, gold mines, farms, factories, steamships, theaters, department stores and radio stations that he owns.

"I've invested in practically every business there is," he told Donald. Uncle Scrooge is the world's biggest investor, with bank accounts, stocks and bonds and other liquid sources of wealth. A good investor puts his money to work! As he told his nephews, "Saving money is the first important step to wealth . . . but I hope you realize I didn't get to be the world's richest duck just by salting my money away!"

How To Use the Scrooge Philosophy To Make Money

Like most Disney cartoons and comic books, Uncle Scrooge was not written solely for children's entertainment. It has many applications for adults. As I see it, the Scrooge philosophy is threefold:

- Look for bargain opportunities to make money.

- Always be cost conscious; make the most for every penny you spend.
- Always do your homework; go out and check the facts yourself.

There's a little bit of Scrooge in all of us. You may not be a miser or self-centered, but you want to keep as much of your wealth as possible. The Scrooge philosophy is simple: The less you have to pay others, the more you keep for yourself! That is the essential theme behind this book.

In the investment world, saving money on commissions, fees and other costs can make a big difference in what you keep. My findings demonstrate that by shopping around and selecting the right investment, broker or banker, you can literally put thousands of dollars more in your pocket each year! I've broken down each investment area—including stocks, bonds, gold, cash, collectibles and foreign investments—to prove that you can save thousands of dollars in each category.

You do not have to read each chapter in order. Feel free to go to any investment area you are interested in, and you'll see how much you can save.

The world's most successful businesspeople and investors have always been bargain hunters. They avoid paying too much, whether it be for a business, a stock or a collectible. Men like John D. Rockefeller, J. Paul Getty or Warren Buffett were always cost conscious. Why? Because if costs get out of hand, a thriving business can quickly become unprofitable.

As economists have shown time and time again, whether a business or investment is profitable depends on the margin. Those always on the lookout to eliminate unnecessary costs are the ones who survive recessions and outperform their competitors.

Even millionaires can go bankrupt because they don't watch their costs and end up spending money foolishly. "A small leak can sink a great ship," Benjamin Franklin once said.

It's not how much you make, it's how much you keep that matters. If you watch your costs closely, you'll be ahead of the crowd.

Don't Be Penny-Wise and Pound-Foolish

This is not to say that you should be penny-wise and pound-foolish. There's nothing wrong with paying more for something, as long as you get value for what you pay. A full-service broker may offer valuable information that a discount broker doesn't have. A stock or mutual fund that you have to pay a broker to buy may far outperform a no-load mutual fund. Expertise has its price. But just make sure you don't pay for it dearly. Follow Uncle Scrooge's dictum: Always use the cheapest way to get what you want! Pay what is necessary and no more!

Uncle Scrooge was never a passive investor, and neither should you be. Always be active and up-to-date, and you will succeed like never before in your business and your portfolio. Uncle Scrooge never relied on magic or mechanistic formulas to get rich, and neither should you. There is no substitute for hard work.

We hope this special book will help you along the way.

Happy bargain hunting, all you investment misers!

CHAPTER I

Cut the Cost of Holding Cash

Ready money is Aladdin's lamp.

—LORD BYRON

EVEN HOLDING something as simple as cash has a cost. These costs usually aren't large, and they may even escape your notice. But, as all wise misers know, those nickels and dimes add up. As Benjamin Franklin popularized the phrase, "A penny saved is a penny earned."

You may recall pictures of Uncle Scrooge's vault, filled with gold and silver coins and greenbacks stacked 100 feet high. Such a hoard makes little sense today! (Although, it is smart to keep a bag or two of gold, silver and cash in case of a national emergency or a banking crisis.)

$ COST-CUTTING TIP #1
Don't Hold Too Many Greenbacks

When you hold greenbacks—cold, hard cash—in your personal possession, there is a substantial cost. It is what the economists call *opportunity cost*. The opportunity cost is the amount you give up by not having that money at work, earning interest.

If you keep a lot of cash stuffed in a mattress, or even in a safe-deposit box, you're not even breaking even; you're losing money. Inflation is slowly eating away at the value of your savings. That's one reason I don't recommend holding anything more than a few thousand dollars in greenbacks. Another reason is that large amounts of cash are often viewed as a lure to thieves or even as a sign of criminal activity—like drug dealing.

You're far better off keeping most of your cash in an interest-bearing account of some type—even a 5% passbook savings account—than socked away where it's not earning anything. But you can do better than 5%. . . .

$ COST-CUTTING TIP #2
Get the Lowest-Cost, Highest-Yielding Money Fund

Comparison shopping among money market funds could be an incredibly tedious and time-consuming endeavor. There are some 742 of them, all with different portfolios, expense ratios, checking privileges, tax statuses and other features. Imagine the difficulty you would have in ordering prospectuses from all those firms, studying them and plotting the differences.

Fortunately, someone has already done all that for you. The most comprehensive source of information on money market funds available is the *IBC Donoghue's Money Fund Directory*. Copies may be on the shelf in your local library. If not, you can order a copy ($27.95 postpaid) by writing or calling: IBC Directory, 290 Eliot St., Ashland, MA 01721, 800/343-5413.

Better yet, every Monday, the *Wall Street Journal* ($0.75 per copy) lists the latest yields on money market funds. You can also get a *free* copy of *Donoghue's Top Money Funds*, a quarterly report that lists the top-ten taxable money funds, the top-ten tax-free money funds, the top-ten state tax-free money funds, the top-ten money funds with check-writing privileges ($100 or less minimum) and the top-ten by yield. Call Donoghue's toll-free, 24-hour hotline to order: 800/445-5900.

$ COST-CUTTING TIP #3
Invest in Money Funds with Low Expense Ratios

The highest-yielding funds are generally those with the *lowest expense ratio*, the ratio that compares mutual fund expenses for management and other overhead expenses to average net asset value.

Expense ratios on money funds can range widely—from 0.25% to 1.69%. Two of the funds with the lowest expense ratios are GW (Great Western) Sierra Global Money Market Fund (800/331-3426, in California, 800/221-9876 except in Los Angeles, 213/488-2200) and Vanguard Money Market Reserve Prime (P.O. Box 2600, Valley Forge, PA 19482, 800/662-7447 or 215/648-6000). Their expense ratios are 0.25% and 0.30%, respectively.

$ COST-CUTTING TIP #4
Invest in Money Funds That Waive Their Fees

At least two money market funds either partially or fully waive their fees. This is a marketing strategy to draw in customers, but if it saves you money, who cares? The two are the Dreyfus Worldwide Dollar Money Market Fund (800/782-6620 or 718/895-1206) and the Fidelity Spartan Money Market Fund (800/544-8888 or 617/523-1919).

At this writing, Dreyfus has waived its management fee several times in the past and is likely to do so again. Fidelity Spartan is only waiving its fee partially, but it still means a greater yield for you. It guarantees that its management fee will not go above 0.45%, which is one of the lowest available, through 1995. Of that amount, Fidelity is currently absorbing all but 0.15%. The percentage absorbed will decline in small increments between now and the end of 1995. But even at the full 0.45%, it will still be one of the relatively low-cost money funds.

Of course, Dreyfus and Fidelity aren't the only money market funds currently waiving their fees—they're just the ones that have been most widely advertised. Other funds may waive their fees for a time. It pays to watch the advertising in various financial publications or in the business section of your local newspaper to find them.

Most money funds require minimum checks of at least $250. Even most banks impose fees on checking accounts. However, one money fund will give you free, unlimited check-writing privileges. The minimum investment is only $100, with minimum additional investments of only $20.

The fund is United Services U.S. Treasury Securities Cash. For information, contact: United Services Advisors, Inc., P.O. Box 29467, San Antonio, TX 78229, 800/873-8637 or 512/523-2453. A $5 fee is charged on every telephone switch to 1 of the other 12 funds in the United Services family. You can get around this, of course, by writing a check to the other fund rather than switching by phone.

My longtime readers know that I dislike investing in U.S. government securities. As far as I'm concerned, it's money thrown down the drain. All it does is fund and encourage wasteful government spending. I much prefer to invest my money in the private sector, where it's actually doing some good. So this fund is only recommended for those whose conscience allows them to invest in the U.S. government. The same goes for the next cost-cutting tip.

$ COST-CUTTING TIP #5
Buy T-Bills Directly from Uncle Sam

If you buy Treasury bills (T-bills) through a bank or broker, you'll have to pay $35 to $60 for each transaction. If you sell before maturity, you'll pay that amount again. But you can buy T-bills and other Treasury securities directly from the federal government, through its Treasury Direct program, completely eliminating fees and commission charges. Clearly, buying directly from Uncle Sam can save money. But there are several potential problems:

- You must purchase at least $10,000 worth and buy in multiples of $5,000 above that minimum. That's above the head of most investors.

- You do not receive an actual engraved certificate; T-bills are simply book-entry securities. The government is not set up to sell your T-bills before maturity, and since there's no actual bill to sell, you can't sell through a broker either. As far as I can tell, you're stuck with your T-bill until maturity, which will be 13, 26 or 52 weeks from the date of purchase, depending on which maturity bill you've chosen. If there's any possibility you will need to sell before maturity, do not buy through the government. Invest with either a broker or a T-bill money market fund.

- Buying through the government can be a major headache if you want to pay with a check from your money market fund. The government only accepts a certified personal or cashier's check. Likewise, in receiving your interest payments or in receiving your funds at maturity, it will be a major headache trying to get your money sent to a money market fund account. The Treasury apparently allows payments only from banks. You can, however, automatically roll over, or reinvest, your money each time your T-bill matures, for up to two years. Simply check the appropriate box when you fill out your Treasury Direct account form. Allow only payments to banks.

However, there is one big tax-planning advantage that might offset these hassles. Treasury bills do not pay regular interest the way, say, a bank or money market account does. Rather, they are sold at a *discount*, based on the prevailing interest rate, and then you are paid the full amount at maturity. If the T-bills you buy today do not come due until next year, you can postpone taxes on the interest until then. In T-bill money market funds, interest is generally posted monthly, and it's taxable in the year you receive it.

▶ *Action To Take:* For more information on Treasury Direct, call or write: Bureau of Public Debt, Division of Customer Services, 1300 C Street, S.W., Washington, D.C. 20239, 202/287-4113. Or get in touch with 1 of the 37 Federal Reserve Bank branches nearest you (see table 1.1).

TABLE 1.1
Addresses and Telephone Numbers of Federal Reserve Banks
and Treasury Servicing Offices

For In-Person Visits	*For Written Correspondence*
Atlanta	
104 Marietta Street, N.W.	FRB Atlanta
Atlanta, GA	104 Marietta Street, N.W.
404/521-8653	Atlanta, GA 30303
404/521-8657 (recording)	
Baltimore	
502 South Sharp Street	Baltimore Branch
Baltimore, MD	FRB of Richmond
301/576-3553	P.O. Box 1378
301/576-3500 (recording)	Baltimore, MD 21203
Birmingham	
1801 Fifth Avenue, North	Birmingham Branch
Birmingham, AL	FRB Atlanta
205/731-8702	P.O. Box 830447
	Birmingham, AL 35283-0447
Boston	
600 Atlantic Avenue	FRB of Boston
Boston, MA	P.O. Box 2076
617/973-3810	Boston, MA 02106
617/973-3805 (recording)	
Buffalo	
160 Delaware Avenue	Buffalo Branch
Buffalo, NY	FRB of New York
716/849-5079	P.O. Box 961
716/849-5030 (recording)	Buffalo, NY 14240
Charlotte	
530 East Trade Street	Charlotte Branch
Charlotte, NC	FRB of Richmond
704/358-2410 or 2411	P.O. Box 30248
704/358-2424 (recording)	Charlotte, NC 28230
Chicago	
230 South LaSalle Street	FRB of Chicago
Chicago, IL	P.O. Box 834
312/322-5369	Chicago, IL 60690
312/786-1110 (recording)	

TABLE 1.1
Addresses and Telephone Numbers of Federal Reserve Banks
and Treasury Servicing Offices (*continued*)

For In-Person Visits	*For Written Correspondence*
Cincinnati 150 East Fourth Street Cincinnati, OH 513/721-4787, ext. 333	Cincinnati Branch FRB of Cleveland P.O. Box 999 Cincinnati, OH 45201
Cleveland 1455 East Sixth Street Cleveland, OH 216/579-2490	FRB of Cleveland P.O. Box 6387 Cleveland, OH 44101
Dallas 400 South Akard Street Dallas, TX 214/651-6362 214/651-6177 (recording)	FRB of Dallas Securities Dept. Station K Dallas, TX 75222
Denver 1020 16th Street Denver, CO 303/572-2477 303/572-2475 (recording)	Denver Branch FRB of Kansas City P.O. Box 5228 Terminal Annex Denver, CO 80217
Detroit 160 West Fort Street Detroit, MI 313/964-6157 313/963-4936 (recording)	Detroit Branch FRB of Chicago P.O. Box 1059 Detroit, MI 48231
El Paso 301 East Main Street El Paso, TX Call Dallas 214/651-6362 214/651-6177 (recording)	El Paso Branch FRB of Dallas P.O. Box 100 El Paso, TX 79999

Helena
The Helena Branch of the Federal Reserve Bank of Minneapolis does not deal in
Treasury securities. Persons in the area served by the Helena Branch should
instead contact the Minneapolis office listed on page 17.

TABLE 1.1
**Addresses and Telephone Numbers of Federal Reserve Banks
and Treasury Servicing Offices (*continued*)**

For In-Person Visits	*For Written Correspondence*
Houston	
1701 San Jacinto Street	Houston Branch
Houston, TX	FRB of Dallas
713/659-4433	P.O. Box 2578
713/652-1688 (recording)	Houston, TX 77252
Jacksonville	
800 West Water Street	Jacksonville Branch
Jacksonville, FL	FRB of Atlanta
904/632-1179	P.O. Box 2499
	Jacksonville, FL 32231-2499
Kansas City	
925 Grand Avenue	FRB of Kansas City
Kansas City, MO	Attn. Securities Dept.
816/881-2783 or 2409	P.O. Box 419440
816/881-2767 (recording)	Kansas City, MO 64141-6440
Little Rock	
325 West Capitol Avenue	Little Rock Branch
Little Rock, AR	FRB of St. Louis
501/372-5451, ext. 288	P.O. Box 1261
	Little Rock, AR 72203
Los Angeles	
950 South Grand Avenue	Los Angeles Branch
Los Angeles, CA	FRB of San Francisco
213/624-7398	P.O. Box 2077
213/688-0068 (recording)	Terminal Annex
	Los Angeles, CA 90051
Louisville	
410 South Fifth Street	Louisville Branch
Louisville, KY	FRB of St. Louis
502/568-9236 or 9231	P.O. Box 32710
	Louisville, KY 40232
Memphis	
200 North Main Street	Memphis Branch
Memphis, TN	FRB of St. Louis
901/523-7171	P.O. Box 407
Ext. 622 or 629	Memphis, TN 38101
Ext. 641 (recording)	

TABLE 1.1
Addresses and Telephone Numbers of Federal Reserve Banks and Treasury Servicing Offices (*continued*)

For In-Person Visits	*For Written Correspondence*

Miami
9100 N.W. 36th Street
Miami, FL
305/471-6497

Miami Branch
FRB of Atlanta
P.O. Box 520847
Miami, FL 33152-0847

Minneapolis
250 Marquette Avenue
Minneapolis, MN
612/340-2075

FRB of Minneapolis
P.O. Box 491
Minneapolis, MN 55480

Nashville
301 Eighth Avenue, North
Nashville, TN
615/251-7100

Nashville Branch
FRB of Atlanta
301 Eighth Avenue, North
Nashville, TN 37203

New Orleans
525 St. Charles Avenue
New Orleans, LA
504/586-1505
Ext. 293 or 294

New Orleans Branch
FRB of Atlanta
P.O. Box 61630
New Orleans, LA 70161

New York
33 Liberty Street
New York, NY
212/720-6619 (recording)
212/720-5823 (results)
212/720-7773 (new offerings)

FRB of New York
Federal Reserve P.O. Station
New York, NY 10045

Oklahoma City
226 Dean A. McGee Avenue
Oklahoma City, OK
405/270-8652

Oklahoma City Branch
FRB of Kansas City
P.O. Box 25129
Oklahoma City, OK 73125

Omaha
2201 Farnam Street
Omaha, NE
402/221-5636

Omaha Branch
FRB of Kansas City
P.O. Box 3958
Omaha, NE 68102

TABLE 1.1

Addresses and Telephone Numbers of Federal Reserve Banks
and Treasury Servicing Offices (*continued*)

For In-Person Visits	For Written Correspondence
Philadelphia	
Ten Independence Mall	FRB of Philadelphia
Philadelphia, PA	P.O. Box 90
215/574-6675 or 6680	Philadelphia, PA 19105-0090
Pittsburgh	
717 Grant Street	Pittsburgh Branch
Pittsburgh, PA	FRB of Cleveland
412/261-7863	P.O. Box 867
412/261-7988 (recording)	Pittsburgh, PA 15230-0867
Portland	
915 S.W. Stark Street	Portland Branch
Portland, OR	FRB of San Francisco
503/221-5932	P.O. Box 3436
503/221-5921 (recording)	Portland, OR 97208-3436
Richmond	
701 East Byrd Street	FRB of Richmond
Richmond, VA	P.O. Box 27622
804/697-8372	Richmond, VA 23261-7622
804/697-8355 (recording)	
Salt Lake City	
120 South State Street	Salt Lake City Branch
Salt Lake City, UT	FRB of San Francisco
801/322-7944	P.O. Box 30780
801/322-7911 (recording)	Salt Lake City, UT 84130
San Antonio	
126 East Nueva Street	San Antonio Branch
San Antonio, TX	FRB of Dallas
512/978-1305 or 1309	P.O. Box 1471
512/978-1330 (recording)	San Antonio, TX 78295
San Francisco	
101 Market Street	FRB of San Francisco
San Francisco, CA	P.O. Box 7702
415/974-2330	San Francisco, CA 94120-7702
415/974-3491 (recording)	

TABLE 1.1
Addresses and Telephone Numbers of Federal Reserve Banks
and Treasury Servicing Offices (*continued*)

For In-Person Visits	*For Written Correspondence*
Seattle	
1015 Second Avenue	Seattle Branch
Seattle, WA	FRB of San Francisco
206/343-3605	P.O. Box 3567
206/343-3615 (recording)	Terminal Annex
	Seattle, WA 98124
St. Louis	
411 Locust Street	FRB of St. Louis
St. Louis, MO	P.O. Box 442
314/444-8665 or 8666	St. Louis, MO 63166
314/444-8602 (recording)	
United States Treasury	
Washington, D.C.	
Bureau of the Public Debt	Mail inquiries to:
1300 C Street, S.W.	Bureau of the Public Debt
Washington, D.C.	Washington, D.C. 20239-1000
202/287-4113	
Device for hearing impaired:	Mail tenders to:
202/287-4097	Bureau of the Public Debt
	Washington, D.C.
	20239-1500

$ COST-CUTTING TIP #6
A T-Bill Fund with a Tax-Advantage Twist

If you have to invest in T-bills, perhaps the best way is with a T-bill fund that defers current taxation and thus helps you keep your tax money out of Uncle Sam's pocket. That's the Permanent Portfolio Treasury Bill Portfolio.

Like most money funds, it charges no commission and offers check-writing privileges. It only invests in short-term Treasury securities.

Unlike other T-bill funds, however, it doesn't declare a daily dividend. Rather, it reinvests its earnings, so that share value increases every day. This means that the earnings you receive are not taxed until you redeem your shares—and only for the shares that you redeem.

It's a clever concept, but it has a few drawbacks. First, there's a fee of $1.00 for each check you write. Second, there's an account maintenance fee of $1.50 per month. Third, it has an unavoidable $35.00 start-up fee.

This fund is best for people who maintain large balances in their money fund, as an alternative to a savings account. It can also be used for estate planning, as shares that you don't redeem during your lifetime can be passed on to heirs, free of income tax.

For more information, contact: Permanent Portfolio Family of Funds, P.O. Box 5847, Austin, TX 78763, 800/531-5142 or 512/453-7558.

$ COST-CUTTING TIP #7
The Lowest-Cost, Short-Term Global Income Fund

At first glance, the Blanchard Short-Term Global Income Fund looks like a money fund. It is no load and offers free check writing ($250 minimum). It's currently yielding over 9%.

The fund invests in short-term money market instruments in the U.S. dollar and foreign currencies, capturing the higher yields offered by some countries. The fund hedges its portfolio against adverse currency moves.

However, you should consider some risks and costs. First, there is some risk to your principal. The net asset value of the fund could decline, wiping out some of that extra yield you're getting. Michael Freedman, president of the Blanchard Group of Funds, puts the possible share fluctuation at plus or minus 3% annually, based on the past performance of similar funds.

Currently, a portion of the management fee is being waived, although, according to the registration statement, the waiver "may be rescinded at any time without notice to shareholders." There is also a one-time account opening fee, but you can get around this by investing in the Blanchard money market fund, and then switching to the Global Income Fund.

For more information, contact: Blanchard Group of Funds, 41 Madison Ave., 24th Fl., New York, NY 10010, 800/688-7904 or 212/779-7979. Minimum investment: $3,000.

CHAPTER 2

Bargains for the Stock Buyer

I got rich because I always made my own lucky breaks.

—UNCLE SCROOGE MCDUCK

ACCORDING TO a survey in the *Wall Street Journal*, it's getting more expensive to be an investor. Major brokerage firms are raising commissions and nickel and diming customers to death with higher handling fees.

According to the survey, in 1990, several major Wall Street firms—Dean Witter, Merrill Lynch, Smith Barney, PaineWebber and Prudential-Bache—raised their commissions. Other firms kept their commissions level but raised their handling charges.

It's time for investors to consider alternatives. If you do most of your own research or get your recommendations from newsletters and other sources, consider a discount broker (see chap. 3). But even if you use a full-service broker, you can cut your costs substantially in several ways.

$ COST-CUTTING TIP #8
Negotiate Discounts of Up to 20% from Your Full-Service Broker

If you have a large or active account, generating over $5,000 in commissions a year, you may be able to negotiate a discount. This is especially true if you don't consume a lot of your broker's time calling for quotes, discussing investments and requesting research. Then, a 10% to 20% discount may be in order.

$ COST-CUTTING TIP #9
Consider Merrill Lynch's Blueprint Plan

I'm not a fan of Merrill Lynch. In fact, in 1990, I told my readers to consider closing their accounts there in protest against the firm's decision to forbid clients to buy South African stocks. What right do they have to ban the investment choices of their clients? They're supposed to serve their clients, not lecture them about South African politics.

However, in the interest of providing comprehensive information, I will mention one of their programs. It's called the Blueprint Program. For $30 a year, you can get moderate discounts on their brokerage service. It's geared to the small investor. (Larger investors should go elsewhere.)

For more information, contact: Merrill Lynch Blueprint Program, P.O. Box 30441, New Brunswick, NJ 08989, 800/637-3766.

$ COST-CUTTING TIP #10
Eliminate Commissions with
Dividend Reinvestment Plans

About 1,000 U.S. companies offer *dividend reinvestment plans* (*DRIPs*), which allow current shareholders to buy stock without paying any commission or other transaction costs. Many of these firms (about 140) allow you to buy these shares at a discount, sometimes up to 10% off the market price. Typically, though, the discount is 2.5% to 5%. Companies that give you 3% to 5% discounts include UtiliCorp United, Fleet/Norstar Financial, Security Pacific, MNC Financial,

Signet Banking, Citizens & Southern, Bank of Boston, Citicorp and
J. P. Morgan. Some plans even allow you to make additional cash
purchases directly from the company. However, purchases are usually
restricted to a certain amount.

The terms for establishing and maintaining a DRIP account differ
between firms; you'll have to check with the individual companies to
see what their programs are. Some of the U.S. companies offering
DRIPs are found in table 2.1.

TABLE 2.1
Top U.S. Companies Offering DRIPs

A
Abbott Laboratories
Aetna Life & Casualty
Alco Standard
Allegheny Power System
American Brands
American Business Corp.
American Family Corp.
American General
American Heritage Life
American Home Products
American Water Works
AMP
AmSouth Bancorp
Anheuser-Busch
Aon
Ashland Oil
Atlanta Gas Light
Atlantic Energy
Avery International

B
Ball
Baltimore Gas & Electric
Bank of America
Bank of New York
Banc One
Bank of Boston
Bank South
Bankers Trust
Banta
Barnett Banks

Baxter International
BB&T Financial
Becton, Dickinson
Black Hills
Boatman's Bancshares
Bob Evan's Farms
Borden
Bristol-Myers Squibb
Brooklyn Union Gas
Browning-Ferris Industries
Brush Wellman

C
California Water Service
Campbell Soup
Capital Holding
Carlisle Companies
CCB Financial
Central Maine Power Co.
Central Fidelity Banks
Century Telephone Enterprises
Chase Manhattan Bank
Chemical Bank
Chubb Group
Cincinnati Bell
Cincinnati Financial
Citicorp
Citizens & Southern
Clorox
Coca-Cola
Colgate-Palmolive
Colonial Gas

TABLE 2.1
Top U.S. Companies Offering DRIPs (*continued*)

ConAgra
Connecticut Water Service
Consolidated Edison Co. of NY
Consolidated Natural Gas
Consumers Water
CoreStates Financial
Crompton & Knowles
Curtice Burns Foods

D
Dana Corp.
Dayton Hudson
Dean Foods
Delmarva Power & Light
Disney (Walt)
Dominion Bankshares
Dominion Resources
Donnelley (R. R.) & Sons
Dow Jones & Co.
Duke Power

E
E'town
Emerson Electric
EnergyNorth
Equifax

F
Federated-Mogul Corp.
First Alabama Bancshares
First Interstate Bancorp
First Michigan Bank
First Tennessee National
First Third Bancorp
First Union
First Virginia Banks
Firstar
Fleet/Norstar Financial Group
Florida Progress
Flowers Industries
FPL Group

G
Gannett
General Cinema

General Electric
General Signal Products
Gerber Products
Gillette
Gorman-Rupp
Grace (W. R.) & Co.
Green Mountain Power
GTE

H
Hannaford Brothers Co.
Harsco Corp.
Hartford Steam Boiler
Hawaiian Electric Industries
Heinz
Hershey Foods
Honeywell
Hormel & Co.
Hospital Corp. of America
Hubbell
Humana
Huntington Bancshares
Hydraulic

I
IE Industries
IBM
Indiana Energy
Iowa-Illinois Gas & Electric
Iowa Resources

J
Jefferson-Pilot
Johnson & Johnson
Johnson Controls
Jostens

K
Kansas Power & Light
Kellog Co.
KeyCorp
Keystone International
Kimberly-Clark
Knight-Ridder

TABLE 2.1
Top U.S. Companies Offering DRIPs (*continued*)

L
La-Z-Boy Chair
Laclede Gas
Lance
Landmark Bancshares
LG&E Energy
Lilly (Eli) & Co.
Louisiana-Pacific
Luby's Cafeterias

M
Madison Gas & Electric
Mark Twain Bancshares
Marsh & McLennan Cos.
Marshall & Illsley
Martin Marietta
McDonald's
McGraw-Hill
Mercantile Bankshares
Merck & Co.
Meridian Bancorp
Middlesex Water
Millipore
Minnesota Mining & Manufacturing
Minnesota Power & Light
MNC Financial
Monsanto
Morgan (J. P.) & Co.

N
National Medical Enterprises
National Service Industries
NBD Bancorp
NCNB
Nevada Power
New Jersey Resources
New Plan Realty Trust
New York Times
Nordson
North Carolina Natural Gas
Northern States Power
Northwest Natural Gas
Nucor

O
Ohio Casualty
Oklahoma Gas & Electric
Olin Orange & Rockland Utilities
Otter Tail Power

P
Pennsylvania Power & Light
Pentair
PepsiCo
Pfizer
Philip Morris
Piedmont Natural Gas
PNC Financial
Potomac Electric Power
PPG Industries
Premier Industrial
Primark Corp.
Procter & Gamble
Public Service Enterprise Group

Q
Quaker Oats Co.
Questar

R
Ralston Purina
Rochester Telephone
Rockwell International
Rouse RPM, Inc.
Rubbermaid Inc.

S
Saint Joseph Light & Power
St. Paul Companies
Sara Lee
SCANA
SCEcorp
Security Bancorp
Security Pacific
Selective Insurance Group
Sherwin-Williams
Signet Banking
Smucker (J. M.)
Society

TABLE 2.1
Top U.S. Companies Offering DRIPs (*continued*)

South Carolina National	**V**
South Jersey Industries	Valley Bancorporation
Southern California Water	Valley National Bancorp (NJ)
Southern Indiana G&E	Valley Resources
Southern New England	VF Corp.
Telecommunications	
SouthTrust	**W**
Southwest Water	Wachovia
Stanley Works	Walgreen
Star Banc	Warner-Lambert
State Street Boston	Washington Energy
Summit Bancorporation	Washington Gas Light
Super Valu Stores	Washington R.E.I.T.
Synovus Financial	Waste Management
	Weis Markets
T	Whitman
Telephone & Data Systems	Winn-Dixie Stores
Texas Utilities	Wisconsin Energy
Thomas & Betts	Witco
TNP Enterprises	Worthington Industries
	WPL Holdings
U	
Union Electric	**Z**
Universal	Zero
USLIFE	
UST	
Utilicorp United	

Several Canadian firms also offer DRIPs. Table 2.2 shows some that currently trade on the Toronto Stock Exchange.

TABLE 2.2
Canadian Firms Offering DRIPs

Alberta Energy	CIBC
Alcan	Consolidated Bathurst
Bank of Montreal	CP Ltd.
Bank of Nova Scotia	Dofasco
BC Telephone	Imasco
Bell Enterprises	Imperial Oil
Bramalea Ltd.	Inco
Bruncor	Intercity Gas
Canadian Development Corp.	Interprov. Pipe Line

TABLE 2.2
Canadian Firms Offering DRIPs (*continued*)

IU International	Nova
John Labatt Ltd.	Quebec Telephone
Maritime T & T	Royal Bank
Molson Cos.	Royal Trustco
Moore Corp.	Stelco
National Bank	Toronto-Dominion Bank
Noranda	TransAlta Utilities
Norcen	TransCanada Pipe Lines
Northern Telecom	Westcoast Transmission

Complete listings of DRIPs are available from Evergreen Enterprises, P.O. Box 763, Laurel, MD 20725, $28.95 per copy.

$ COST-CUTTING TIP #11
Buy Stocks Commission-Free
from the First Share

Voluntary investment plans (VIPs) are like DRIPs for new shares. Some companies allow you to buy large quantities of stock, commission-free, if you hold as little as one share of a stock. For example, if you own one share of Phillips Petroleum, you can buy $120,000 worth of the company's stock without paying one penny in commission. Other major companies, like Martin Marietta and Philip Morris, offer similar plans.

An even better deal is to invest with one of the few companies that allows you to buy every share directly from the company itself, including your very first share. The best company that currently offers such a plan is Procter & Gamble (NYSE: PG). Commissions—if you can call them that—run a paltry $0.08 per share (less than 0.1% of the stock's current value). Minimum to start: one share. For an application, write: P&G Shareholder Services, 1 Procter & Gamble Plaza, Cincinnati, OH 45202, or call: 800/742-6253, in Ohio, 800/582-2685 or 513/983-3413.

$ COST-CUTTING TIP #12
Eight Common-Sense Cautions
in Buying New Issues

One of the advantages of buying a new issue is that the broker does not charge a commission. (He's paid by the underwriter.) But new issues have some hidden dangers. Remember, the firm is making the offering to make money. So it wants to get as much as it can for its shares.

Some *initial public offerings (IPOs)* perform phenomenally well, and the initial offering price is a bargain (or a blockbuster). Consider what happened to Home Shopping Network. When it went public in 1986, at $18, the stock soared to $42 5/8 on the first day! It then jumped as high as $133, before splitting three-for-one. In more recent years, however, the stock has plunged to below $3!

According to a recent survey in *Forbes*, most new issues rise initially but sell below their offering price two years later. As you can see, IPOs can give you a wild ride. Here are eight guidelines for finding the bargains and staying away from those that are overpriced.

- Be careful in a booming market. The highest-price offerings come with a red-hot market. You'll be better off waiting until the market cools down before you buy a long-term position.
- Watch out for low-price shares. Anything under $10 should be considered speculative—and generally, the lower the price the more speculative it is.
- Make sure the company isn't just a fad investment.
- Be careful of start-ups. Usually, it's less risky to invest in IPOs that have a solid operating history as private companies.
- Make sure most of the money raised in the IPO will be used to expand the company, not just for securities investment or to repay debt. Be especially careful if a large percentage of the shares are being sold by a founding shareholder.
- Make sure that the current management team is the one responsible for the company's success. If not, find out if the current management has a successful track record in the industry.

- Avoid stocks that have jumped 50% or more in price in the first few days. Those stocks often are targeted by short sellers and that puts a damper on further price gains.
- Look for stocks that have only risen 10% to 20% in the first few days. Such a rise indicates strong investor interest but rarely captures the attention of short sellers.

$ COST-CUTTING TIP #13
Buy Closed-End Funds at Discounts of Up to 40%!

Closed-end funds are a great way to hunt for stock market bargains. These funds are investment companies that hold a portfolio of stocks, bonds, gold or other assets and then issue a fixed number of shares. They trade on a stock exchange just like a share of IBM or General Motors. Hundreds of them are available, and they often trade at a discount to their *net asset value (NAV)*. *Barron's* and the *Wall Street Journal* list them each week.

These funds often trade for less than the value of the underlying assets in the fund. I've seen these discounts widen to as much as 40%, as in the case of Convertible Holdings (NYSE: CNV). However, spreads that large are rare, and they don't usually last long. A good rule of thumb is that once a fund gets near an 18% to 20% discount, it merits serious consideration. The Closed-End Funds section of *Barron's* each week indicates the discount for each fund.

It's critical to look at the fund's management, as well as the prospects for the underlying investments. Many closed-end funds, for example, are country funds that invest in the stocks of a single country, like Brazil, Korea, Thailand, Germany or Great Britain. If you aren't optimistic about that country's stock market, it doesn't make sense to buy the fund, even if it is selling at a high discount.

$ COST-CUTTING TIP #14
For an Even Greater Discount, Buy a
Closed-End Fund with a DRIP

Some closed-end funds offer DRIPs. These funds usually allow you the option of reinvestment at lower than market price or NAV but not less than 95% of the market price. Some of the closed-end funds currently offering DRIPs include Gabelli Equity Trust, Liberty All-Star, Royce Value Trust, Growth Stock Outlook Trust and Comstock Partners, all trading on the New York Stock Exchange (NYSE).

$ COST-CUTTING TIP #15
Avoid New Issues of Closed-End Equity Funds

You are almost always better off avoiding new issues of closed-end equity funds. They are generally offered at their full price, and perhaps even a premium to their NAV, plus a full brokerage commission of 8.5%. Unfortunately, they generally fall to a discount within a few months of their initial offering, so wait for the drop before investing.

A 1989 study of the performance of IPOs of closed-end funds, conducted by the Securities & Exchange Commission (SEC), showed that after 24 weeks, U.S. closed-end equity funds had an average discount of 10%. Foreign stock funds had an average discount of 11.4%. The lesson is clear: If you want to buy a closed-end fund, you're better off waiting until a year or two after the IPO. You'll get the fund at a much greater discount.

Free Closed-End Fund Report

Richard Young, a colleague at Phillips Publishing, recommends A. G. Edwards as the best broker for closed-end funds. The firm publishes a quarterly newsletter, *Closed-End Fund Update*, which contains numbers on dividends, yields, net assets, shares outstanding, and prices and all the other goodies you'll need to keep score on closed-end funds. You can get a free copy by calling Warren Sundstrom, the firm's closed-end fund expert. Dial toll-free: 800/964-1003 or collect: 508/250-0003 and request the latest quarterly edition of *Closed-End Fund Update*.

CHAPTER 3

Which Discount Broker Is Best for You?

Economy is in itself a great source of revenue.

—SENECA

DISCOUNT BROKERS are essential to the Scrooge investor. You can save over 70% in commissions by using discounters instead of full-service brokers. And by carefully shopping among discounters, you can save even more money.

Commission rates vary widely among discounters (see table 3.1). It's not always essential that you choose the lowest-cost discounter. Some of the higher-priced discounters may offer services that more than compensate for the higher commission rates. What is essential is that you choose a discounter that best meets your needs.

Some, for example, offer toll-free quote lines, on-line trading through your personal computer, trading in no-load mutual funds and other services. You'll need to call each of them for a copy of their literature.

$ COST-CUTTING TIP #16
Open an Account with One of the
Big-Three Discount Brokers

Three major discount brokers have offices across the country—Charles Schwab & Co., Fidelity Brokerage and Quick & Reilly. As you can see from the survey in this chapter, all three generally have higher commissions than the other discount brokers. Nevertheless, I believe you should consider opening an account at one of these three.

Chances are, each one has an office near your hometown, particularly if you live in a big city. It's almost always better to deal with a firm that's closer to home. If you have trouble with your account, you can go into the broker's office to work out the problem. If you can't get through on the telephone (as many people couldn't during the 1987 stock market crash), you can go directly to the office to transact your business.

If you travel to other parts of the country, or have a vacation home, these larger discount brokerage firms will likely have an office close to where you are. Also, the larger firms trade no-load and low-load mutual funds; the smaller discount brokers do not.

The following survey shows the amounts charged by seven of my recommended discount brokerage firms. Although the big-three discount brokerage firms have offices across the country, the other four are smaller firms known for their deep discounts or other special services they provide.

Table 3.1 shows the commissions charged by each broker for ten typical transactions.

The addresses and telephone numbers for these discount brokers are:

- Barry W. Murphy & Co., 270 Congress St., Boston, MA 02210, 800/221-2111 or 617/426-1770.
- Charles Schwab & Co., The Schwab Building, 101 Montgomery St., San Francisco, CA 94104, 800/648-5300 or 415/627-7000.
- Fidelity Brokerage Services, Inc., 164 Northern Ave., Boston, MA 02210, 800/544-7272 or 617/570-7000.

- Jack White & Co., Suite 220, 9191 Towne Centre Dr., San Diego, CA 92122, 800/233-3411 or 609/587-2000.
- Kennedy, Cabot & Co., 9465 Wilshire Blvd., Beverly Hills, CA 90212, 800/252-0090 or 213/550-0711.
- Marquette de Bary Co., Inc., 488 Madison Ave., New York, NY 10022, 800/221-3305 or 212/644-5300.
- Quick & Reilly, Inc., 120 Wall Street, New York, NY 10005, 800/221-5220, 212/943-8686, in NY state, 800/522-8712.

TABLE 3.1
Discount Broker Survey

Sample 1: 20,000 Shares @ $0.50 per Share ($10,000)		Sample 2: 5,000 Shares @ $1.00 per Share ($5,000)	
Kennedy, Cabot	$ 200.00	Barry Murphy	$ 75.00
Barry Murphy	225.00	Kennedy, Cabot	75.00
Marquette de Bary	232.00	Marquette de Bary	130.00
Fidelity	300.00	Quick & Reilly	180.00
Jack White	333.00	Jack White	230.00
Quick & Reilly	337.00	Fidelity	258.00
Charles Schwab	439.00	Charles Schwab	270.00

Sample 3: 1,000 Shares @ $5.00 per Share ($5,000)		Sample 4: 100 Shares @ $10.00 per Share ($1,000)	
Barry Murphy	$ 60.00	Marquette de Bary	$ 24.75
Quick & Reilly	60.50	Barry Murphy	28.50
Marquette de Bary	69.85	Kennedy, Cabot	35.00
Jack White	70.00	Jack White	48.00
Kennedy, Cabot	75.00	Charles Schwab	49.00
Charles Schwab	90.00	Quick & Reilly	49.00
Fidelity	90.00	Fidelity	51.00

Sample 5: 1,000 Shares @ $10.00 per Share ($10,000)		Sample 6: 500 Shares @ $20.00 per Share ($10,000)	
Barry Murphy	$ 60.00	Barry Murphy	$ 47.50
Kennedy, Cabot	75.00	Kennedy, Cabot	50.00
Quick & Reilly	84.00	Quick & Reilly	84.00
Jack White	88.00	Jack White	88.00
Charles Schwab	99.00	Marquette de Bary	88.18
Fidelity	104.00	Charles Schwab	99.00
Marquette de Bary	106.81	Fidelity	104.75

TABLE 3.1
Discount Broker Survey (*continued*)

Sample 7: 200 Shares @ $30.00 per Share ($6,000)		Sample 8: 300 Shares @ $40.00 per Share ($12,000)	
Kennedy, Cabot	$ 35.00	Kennedy, Cabot	$ 35.00
Barry Murphy	38.00	Barry Murphy	47.50
Marquette de Bary	54.65	Quick & Reilly	89.00
Quick & Reilly	65.00	Marquette de Bary	91.91
Jack White	74.00	Jack White	94.00
Charles Schwab	87.00	Charles Schwab	105.00
Fidelity	90.75	Fidelity	110.75

Sample 9: 500 Shares @ $50.00 per Share ($25,000)		Sample 10: 300 Shares @ $75.00 per Share ($22,500)	
Kennedy, Cabot	$ 50.00	Kennedy, Cabot	$ 35.00
Barry Murphy	62.50	Barry Murphy	47.50
Quick & Reilly	119.50	Quick & Reilly	115.25
Jack White	133.00	Marquette de Bary	121.09
Charles Schwab	141.00	Jack White	125.50
Marquette de Bary	146.43	Charles Schwab	136.00
Fidelity	148.75	Fidelity	143.75

One note of caution: Calculating commissions can be confusing. If you're ever in doubt about how much the commission will be for a trade, it's a good idea to ask the broker before you place your order. Also, some firms may have changed their commission schedules by the time you read this, so check the current rates.

$ COST-CUTTING TIP #17
Use Barry Murphy for Foreign Stocks

Many discount brokers don't handle foreign stocks. One that does is Barry W. Murphy & Co. Its normal rates on U.S. stocks are quite low. For foreign stocks, Murphy adds a flat $75 charge to normal commissions. Rates for *American depository receipts (ADRs)* are the same as rates for other U.S. stocks.

ADRs are receipts for foreign corporations held in the vault in the foreign branch of a U.S. bank. Many large, foreign corporations sell their stock in the United States in the form of ADRs. They trade over the counter (OTC) just like a U.S. OTC stock. But ADRs are not available for all foreign stocks. In that case, trade directly through Barry W. Murphy & Co.

CHAPTER 4

Saving Money on Mutual Funds

There are few ways in which a man can be more innocently employed than in getting money.

—SAMUEL JOHNSON

MUTUAL FUNDS are, by definition, a low-cost way to get professional management and portfolio diversification. But even here you must keep a watchful eye on commissions and other fees. These are listed at the beginning of every prospectus. Here's a rundown of what they are and how high they can go.

$ COST-CUTTING TIP #18
Minimize the Hidden Fees and Commissions of Mutual Funds

Watch out for *commissions*, also called *loads*. These can range from zero to 8.5%. But that's only part of the story. An 8.5% load is really a 9.3% load, because the commission comes off the top. It reduces the size of the initial investment you make. For example, if you invest $1,000 in an 8.5%-load fund, your initial account will be $915. The $85 commission is 9.3% of $915.

39

Then, there are *management fees*. Typically between 0.5% and 1% annually, they often run higher on some funds.

Next are *12b-1 fees*, named after the SEC rule permitting them. These fees allow funds to pass their distribution and marketing costs on to investors, up to 2%, though most plans charge less than 0.5%. Like the management fee, it's paid to the fund's management annually out of the fund assets. Sometimes funds with 12b-1 fees are touted as no loads, so, here again, it pays to read the prospectus.

To confuse matters further, some funds have *inactive 12b-1 plans*. They have installed the 12b-1 plan just in case they want to impose it in the future, but they aren't implementing it, and it doesn't cost you anything. Again, a careful reading of the prospectus will help.

Redemption fees are sometimes charged to deter active trading. Typically 1% to 2%, they are often rescinded after you've held the fund for six months to a year.

Contingent deferred sales charges—often imposed by large brokerage firms on their no-load funds—can be especially costly. They are charged when you leave the fund. You can pay as much as 5% to 6% if you redeem your shares in the first year, declining by 1% a year for the next five or six years.

$ COST-CUTTING TIP #19
Prefer No-Load and Low-Load Funds

I prefer pure (100%) no-loads funds, though I occasionally recommend low-load funds, up to about 4%. I rarely recommend the higher-commission funds.

Brokers often argue that a higher-commission fund is worth the extra money, because the better performance will make up for the higher load in time. That's absolute nonsense. There's no logical reason why a sales charge, paid to a broker, will result in improved performance of the fund. The broker has nothing to do with how the fund performs.

In fact, the opposite is true. Sheldon Jacobs, author of the *Handbook for No-Load Fund Investors*, points out that "in 1990 the average no-load equity fund lost 6.8% compared to a loss of 7.3% for all equity funds as tracked by the Lipper Mutual Fund Performance Analysis. . . ."

Jacobs's annual *Handbook for No-Load Fund Investors*, by the way, is the most comprehensive source of information available for no-load fund investors, covering 1,304 no-load and low-load funds. At $45, though, it's expensive. So check for it in your local library. To order, call or write: The No-Load Fund Investor, P.O. Box 283, Hastings-on-Hudson, NY 10706, 800/252-2042.

Another drawback to load funds is that it almost forces you to be a long-term investor. If you invest in a load fund and then change your mind, it can be quite costly. *Forbes* ranks mutual funds in a special issue every September, and its honor roll contains both load and no-load funds. *Forbes* found no difference in performance between load and no-load funds.

$ COST-CUTTING TIP #20
Buy the Funds with the
Lowest Management Fee

In general, no-load funds have the lowest management and administrative fees. The average load fund has an expense ratio of 1.4%; the average no-load fund, 1.3%. Higher-fee funds can be expensive in more ways than one. Of course, a higher fee will mean less profits for you. But it can also mean more taxes, since you are required to pay taxes, not just on the dividends you earn, but also on your share of the fund's gross income before management fees.

$ COST-CUTTING TIP #21
Buy No-Load, Low-Fee Index Funds

Index funds invest in a portfolio of securities composing a popular index, in the same proportional quantity as the index. Thus, over time, they will mirror the performance of the index, minus the small administrative fee. Several index funds, for example, buy the stocks comprising the Standard & Poor's (S&P) 500 Index.

TABLE 4.I
Low-Cost Index Funds

Index Fund	Duplicates Composition of	Annual Fee %
Benham Gold Equities (800/4-Safety or 415/965-4274)	30 top North American Gold Stocks	0.75
Bull & Bear FNC Index (800/847-4200 or 212/363-1100)	30 stocks of the Financial News Composite Index	1.53
Dreyfus People's Index (800/645-6561 or 718/895-1206)	S&P 500	0.30
Federated S&P 500 (800/245-2423 or 412/288-1900)	S&P 500	N/A
Fidelity Spartan Market (800/544-8888 or 617/523-1919)	S&P 500	0.45
Gateway Index Plus (800/354-6339 or 513/248-2700)	S&P 100 with options	1.15
Rushmore American Gas Index (800/621-7874 or 301/657-1517)	109 natural gas distribution and transmission companies	0.85
Rushmore Nova	30–50 large capitalization stocks	1.25
Rushmore OTC	100 largest NASDAQ stocks (NASDAQ 100)	1.00
Rushmore Precious Metals	25 major North Am. gold stocks	1.00
Rushmore Stock	80 largest stocks on S&P 100	1.00
United Services All American (800/873-8637 or 512/523-2453)	S&P 500	2.16*
United Services European Equity	Selected stocks in Morgan Stanley Capital Int'l. Index	3.98*
Vanguard Bond Market (800/662-7447 or 215/648-6000)	Salomon Bros. Investment Grade Bond Index	0.21
Vanguard Index Trust Extended Market	4,500 stocks from Wilshire 4,500	0.23
Vanguard International Equity Index—Europe	Morgan Stanley Capital Int'l. (EAFE Index)	0.40
Vanguard International Equity Index—Pacific	Morgan Stanley Capital Int'l. Pacific Index (EAFE Index)	0.35
Vanguard Quantitative Index	S&P 500 using computer models	0.48
Vanguard Index Trust 500 Portfolio	S&P 500	0.22
Vanguard Small Cap	Russell 2,000 Index (smallest companies)	0.31

* These high expense ratios are misleading. They result from one-time expenses in late 1990 to reorganize former funds into index funds. The fund managers are predicting that these expense ratios will be under 2%, eventually going to 1%.

Index funds are much easier to manage than other funds, so their management fees are significantly lower. Check table 4.1, which lists no-load index funds and the indexes they simulate.

Although index funds generally have lower management fees than 'most stock funds, some do impose transaction fees ranging from 0.5% to 1%, which are payable to the fund rather than to the advisor or the sales organization. If you are a holder of the fund, that means the fee is payable to you (and to other investors).

The idea behind such fees is to prevent fund performance from being hurt by the transaction costs connected with purchases and redemptions by shareholders. Without this fee, buy-and-hold investors would be subsidizing much of the transaction costs of those who switch in and out of the fund. Vanguard, for instance, has such a fee in its index funds.

It's important to shop around for an index fund that meets your style of trading. Many index funds have added costs and other restrictions to prevent you from switching in and out of the fund.

Vanguard, for example, does not allow telephone switching into or out of its S&P 500 index fund. You can only redeem shares by sending a letter—and even then, you are limited to two exchanges a year.

United Services charges $5 per switch—not bad for large accounts but a potential problem for the small investor. However, unlike many other index funds, it charges no transaction fee or annual maintenance fee.

If you're not a frequent switcher, the Vanguard funds may be the best deal around. Vanguard, generally, has the lowest expense ratios in the mutual fund industry. However, on some of its index funds, it does charge a 1% transaction fee or a $10 annual maintenance fee.

$ COST-CUTTING TIP #22
Watch for High-Load Fund Families
That Offer Closed-End Funds

A new trend is for fund families that normally charge 5% to 9% loads to offer closed-end funds on the stock exchanges. Closed-end funds trade like stocks on the exchanges. As a result, you can buy them through a discount broker for very little commission, often below 1%, depending on how many shares you want to buy. You can also place a limited-buy order below the current ask; you might get a better deal on the fund. When you buy an open-end fund, you have no choice— you always pay the net asset price plus the 5% to 8% load. Obviously, buying a closed-end fund can save you a lot. Here are several high-load fund families that offer closed-end funds:

- GT Greater Europe Fund (NYSE: GTF): The GT group of funds is one of the top-performing management firms specializing in foreign stocks. You can invest in the GT Europe Fund, an open-end fund that charges a 4.75% load, or you can invest in practically the same thing, without a load, through the GT Greater Europe Fund on the NYSE.
- Templeton Global Income Fund (NYSE: GIM), Templeton Global Government Fund (NYSE: TGG), Templeton Emerging Market Fund (NYSE: EMF) and Templeton Global Utilities (AMEX: TGU): Templeton has an excellent record since his original Templeton Growth Fund came out in 1954. But why pay an 8.5% load when you can buy the above for a small brokerage commission?

$ COST-CUTTING TIP #23
How To Beat Start-Up Fees

Some no-load funds have one-time start-up fees. For example, Terry Coxon's Permanent Portfolio Fund (PPF) has a $35 start-up fee; the Blanchard Global Income Fund has a $75 start-up fee. These are significant expenses, particularly if you're a small investor.

You can sometimes beat these start-up fees by looking at the other funds in the family. Often, they have a money market fund you can invest in at no cost; then you simply switch your money to the other fund. With the Blanchard Global Income Fund, for instance, you can do this, but with the PPF, you cannot. It charges a start-up fee even on its money market fund.

$ COST-CUTTING TIP #24
How To Turn Load Funds
into No-Load Funds

Certain investors may be able to turn some load funds into no-load funds. Again, you'll have to read the prospectus of the fund carefully to find out which classes of people might be exempt from loads.

One fund, for example, the Pacific Horizon Aggressive Growth Fund, exempts people who buy through their employer's thrift plan, those who have opened an IRA at Security Pacific Bank (the fund's sponsor) and those who buy through a discount broker that charges a transaction fee.

Some load funds also eliminate or reduce fees for very large investors—those putting, say, over $1 million into the fund. *Forbes* (September 3, 1990) lists ten top-performing, low-expense funds that offer big investors deep discounts on their loads—some all the way down to zero. These are:

- Cardinal Fund (800/282-9446)
- Fundamental Investors (800/421-9900)
- Lutheran Brotherhood Municipal (800/328-4552)
- Nationwide Fund (800/848-0920)
- New Perspective (800/421-9900)
- Pacific Horizon Aggressive Growth (800/332-3863)
- Templeton Foreign (800/237-0738)
- United Income (800/366-5465)
- United Vanguard (800/366-5465)
- Washington Mutual Investors (800/421-9900)

$ COST-CUTTING TIP #25
Buy Funds for $200, Maximum; Get Paid $100 When You Sell

Jack White & Co., a San Diego-based discount broker, has a service that allows investors to save substantially on commissions when buying certain load funds. White has set up a secondary market for over 200 mutual funds, some of them with hefty loads. For a $200 flat fee, you can buy shares in these funds. No matter how many shares you buy, it's the same fee—$200!

What's more, you can sell without paying commission. In fact, to encourage sellers, White is actually paying *investors* $100 per trade. Not only that, you'll receive the proceeds of the sale within five business days, which is faster than most mutual funds companies generally pay.

Note, however, that this is a new service and has had difficulty in finding sellers of some popular funds. White's scheduled to be listed on the NASDAQ market soon, however, which should enhance liquidity.

$ COST-CUTTING TIP #26
Eliminate the Red Tape in Switching

Some discount brokers (Jack White, Fidelity and Schwab—see chap. 3 on discount brokers for toll-free numbers) trade no-load mutual funds. But why would you pay a commission—even a modest one—to a discount broker to buy or sell no-load funds? The answer is to save time and trouble.

Even though you pay a small commission to buy a no-load fund, you are able to switch easily between families of funds, which normally might take days or weeks, require a certified letter, etc. Also, you can buy through these discount firms without getting a prospectus or account opening form.

$ COST-CUTTING TIP #27
Buy These Funds for Tightwads

Some funds are not only no loads; they are also managed with a Scrooge-like, bargain-hunting philosophy. These fund managers search the stock markets looking for stocks that sell at low *price/ earnings (PE) ratios* and low *book value*. (Book value is the difference between a corporation's assets and its liabilities—theoretically what the company would be worth if it were liquidated.) Of course, a low book value can be a sign of a troubled company—but it can also be the sign of a tremendous bargain.

Here are some *tightwad* funds worth looking at:

- Legg Mason Value Trust, 111 South Calvert St., Baltimore, MD 21202, 800/822-5544 or 301/539-3400. Recommended by my colleague Richard Young, this fund seeks out low price-to-book value stocks. Since inception, in 1982, it has had a total return of 280.6%. It is a no load, with a 0.93% management fee and a 0.15% 12b-1 fee.
- Lindner Fund, 7711 Carondelet 700, St. Louis, MO 63105, 314/ 727-5305. Regularly on *Forbes*'s honor roll of the best gainers of the past five years, it is one of my all-time favorites. It's no load, with low annual expenses of 0.95%.
- Royce Value Fund, 1414 Avenue of the Americas, New York, NY 10019, 800/221-4268 or 212/355-7311. Another fund that takes a value approach to investing. It has a 2.5% front-end load and a 2.5% redemption fee in the first six years. Its annualized return in the eight years since its inception is 11.65%.

Another fund with a different, though equally appealing, Scrooge-like philosophy is Provident Mutual Investment Shares. This fund invests in companies run by tightwads—managements that keep a tight rein on expenses and a constant eye on the bottom line. The fund also has a low portfolio turnover, which means lower transaction fees charged to the fund. Its ten-year average annual return has been a solid 11.7%, after sales charges.

There's only one thing wrong with this fund—the sales charge (6%). It's too bad Scrooge-like investors can't take advantage of this Scrooge-like fund. But, maybe *you* can, if you can get it through Jack White's secondary market.

$ COST-CUTTING TIP #28
Beware of Brokerage Firm Funds

Most *house funds* offered by major stockbrokers are terrible investments. According to a ten-year study by the Boston-based mutual-fund research firm Kanon Bloch Carre & Co., four of the five top Wall Street firms had fund performance results ranging from slightly above average to terrible. Only Merrill Lynch made it into the top-ten fund families.

Part of the reason for this poor performance is the large commissions charged by the big brokers. You automatically start with a 5% to 9% loss through commissions. The two best-performing fund families were the large no-load groups Fidelity and Vanguard.

$ COST-CUTTING TIP #29
Don't Lose with No-Lose Funds

Finally, beware of no-lose mutual funds. Lately, a number of new funds have been promoted that promise the return of your principal after ten years. It's hardly a no-lose proposition. Not only will inflation erode your guarantee, but the funds tend to have high annual administrative fees. The likely result is mediocre performance at best.

CHAPTER 5

The Bargain Hunter's Guide to Higher Income

Conservative investors sleep well.

—PHILIP FISHER

FOR UNCLE Scrooge and anyone else with substantial wealth, earning high income can be more important than earning capital gains. A bird in the hand is worth two in the bush! And the less your broker or fund manager takes out in commissions and fees, the higher the income for you.

Bonds are, of course, the best source for higher income.

But there's good news and bad news about bonds. The good news is that commissions are often low—in some cases, nonexistent. The bad news is that you can still be grossly overcharged by your broker. The reason is markups. The *markup* is the difference between the *bid* price—the price at which brokers will purchase a bond—and the *ask* price—the price at which they will sell that bond to you.

$ COST-CUTTING TIP #30
Buy Bond Funds or Unit Investment Trusts

The market for corporate and municipal bonds tends to be illiquid. A typical bond may trade 30 or 40 times a day, compared to several thousand times for U.S. Treasuries. Ways to keep these markups to a minimum are discussed later in this chapter. But the easiest way—and for many investors the least expensive way—to buy bonds cheaply is through a *bond fund* or a *unit investment trust.*

The median expense ratio on load (commission) bond funds is 0.93%; the median expense ratio on no loads is 0.80%. Obviously, you would want to choose a no-load bond fund.

The Vanguard Group (Valley Forge, PA 19482, 800/662-7447 or 215/648-6000) offers a wide range of bond funds with low expense ratios. The average expense ratios on the Vanguard bond and munici-pal bond funds are 0.35% and 0.25%, respectively—well below the averages for bond funds in general. Vanguard has several bond funds to choose from—municipal, Ginnie Mae, government and corporate, with a variety of maturities.

Another low-cost way of buying bonds is through a unit investment trust. In a unit investment trust, you are sold an undivided interest in a portfolio of bonds. You will receive a proportional share of the net income of the trust and, as the bonds are sold or mature, a return of principal.

The sales load on most unit investment trusts is high—typically 4%. But the high commission is offset by extremely low management fees—around 0.3%. Since unit investment trusts are not actively managed, they generally hold to maturity.

Another advantage of unit investment trusts (and individual bonds) over bond funds is that you have a better chance of getting your principal back. Here's why: If you have a bond fund, and bond prices drop because of rising interest rates, the bond fund may never recover, since it is constantly selling old bonds and buying new ones. (Bond funds do not necessarily hold their bonds to maturity.)

But if you have individual bonds or unit investment trusts, you can hold onto the bonds, and they will eventually go back up as they mature.

One more tip: Sometimes you can find great bargains and high yields from closed-end bond funds that trade on the Big Board and other national exchanges. In my newsletter, I've recommended closed-end bond funds issued by Putnam, Van Kempen, Nuveen, etc. Some have paid double-digit yields plus capital gains. Check the latest *Bar-ron's* or Monday's *Wall Street Journal* for a complete list.

$ COST-CUTTING TIP #31
Try Kemper for a Low-Cost
Unit Investment Trust

Kemper Unit Investment Trusts, a division of Kemper Securities Group, offer several low-cost unit trusts. Some of the current offerings are:

- Tax-free trust: Holds a portfolio of municipal bonds. There is a one-time sales charge of 4.9%. The only other charge is an annual *surveillance fee* of $0.20 for every $1,000 unit.
- Insured corporate trust: Holds a portfolio of insured corporate utility bonds. It has a one-time sales charge of 4.5% and an annual surveillance fee of $0.25 for every $1,000 unit.
- Government securities trust: Several varieties are available, including Ginnie Mae (3.75% sales charge), Fannie Mae (3.00% sales charge) and U.S. Treasury (average life three years, 1.75% sales charge).

You cannot buy these unit trusts directly from Kemper. You must buy them through a broker. For information on the unit trusts or to find out the name of a broker in your area that sells them, contact: Kemper Unit Investment Trusts, 120 S. Riverside Plaza, 6th Fl., Chicago, IL 60606, 800/345-7999 or 312/781-1121.

$ COST-CUTTING TIP #32
Seven Ways To Make Sure the Markup Is Fair

Here are several ways to make sure the markup is fair.

- Always ask your broker what the markup or commission is. Your broker may not like this. He or she may try evading the question. But brokers are required to disclose the markup if you ask. If you can't get a clear answer, go to another broker.

- In most cases, you probably shouldn't pay a markup over 5%. The National Association of Securities Dealers (NASD) generally considers markups of over 5% to be excessive. But this doesn't stop some brokers from charging fees of 8% or higher.
- Find out your brokerage firm's policy on markups in bonds. Some firms have strict rules forbidding excessive markups.
- Compare prices with two other firms. One way to determine the markup is to ask them what price they would buy the bonds for. Then, ask what they would sell them for. The difference between those prices is the markup.
- Don't place *at-market orders* for bonds. This is an order instructing your broker to buy the bond at the market price. If the spread is wide, don't buy right away. Place your order in the middle somewhere, until you get a reasonably priced execution.
- Buy bonds with short- to medium-term maturities. Longer-term bonds (ten years or more to maturity) generally carry commissions three to four times higher than shorter-term bonds.
- Buy higher-quality bonds. The lower-quality bonds are harder for your broker to sell and consequently have higher commissions— sometimes three or four times higher than those on lower-quality bonds.
- Quality, of course, refers primarily to the default risk. Bonds are rated by several independent services, with Moody's being the most popular, on a scale ranging from Aaa (the highest) to D (in default). U.S. Treasury bonds are the highest rated (although sometimes I wonder why, since the federal government's taxing and inflating policy is reaching its limits). Munis and corporate bonds vary widely in their ratings. Anything with a Moody's rating of Ba or lower is considered to be speculative.

There's nothing wrong, of course, with buying lower-quality bonds. I've frequently recommended high-yielding (so-called junk) bonds to my subscribers, depending on the economic climate. The interest rates paid are much higher than that paid on Treasuries. But you should be aware of the risks on higher-yield bonds. (*Moody's Industrial Manual*, which rates bonds, can be found in most libraries.)

$ COST-CUTTING TIP #33
Buy Bonds on Their Initial Offering

Like stocks, bonds are sold commission free in their initial offerings. Prices are low, because of the huge amount of bonds on the market, and the commissions are paid for by the issuer. You also get a prospectus if you buy on the initial offerings—prospectuses are rarely available to buyers in the secondary market.

$ COST-CUTTING TIP #34
Don't Bypass Your Full-Service Broker

Bonds are one investment in which a full-service broker may be cheaper than a discount broker. A discount broker may have to go to a dealer first to buy the bond you want. The dealer will charge a markup. Then, the discounter will put a commission on it, even if it's a small one, before he or she sells it to you. There's no guarantee that your full-service broker will always be cheaper than your discount broker, but it is always worthwhile to check before buying.

Also, don't assume that just because the broker discounts stock commissions he or she won't put a markup on bonds. You should always make sure you know both the bid and the ask price, even when buying from a discounter.

$ COST-CUTTING TIP #35
The Best Discount Brokers for Bonds

Some discount brokers have lower commissions for bonds than others. Phillips Publishing's in-depth report *Investor's Guide to Discount*

Brokers found that when buying corporate or convertible bonds, the discount brokers listed in table 5.1 had the best commission rates, depending on the size of your order.

TABLE 5.1
Best Discounts on Bonds

Number of Bonds	Best Buy
1-5	Barry Murphy (800/221-2111)
	Brown & Co. (800/225-6707)
	Marquette de Bary (800/221-3305)
	Marsh Block (800/366-1500)
	Pacific Brokerage (800/421-8395)
	Stock Cross (800/225-6196)
6–8	Pacific Brokerage (800/421-8395)
9–11	Seaport Securities (800/221-9894)
12–19	Waterhouse Securities (800/327-7500)
20 and up	Kennedy, Cabot & Co. (800/252-0090)

$ COST-CUTTING TIP #36
How To Cut Corners When Buying Zero-Coupon Bonds

Zero-coupon bonds are sometimes called *deeply discounted bonds*. Zeros are bonds that pay no interest but mature at their face value ($1,000). Because of the time value of money, they're sold at a discount to their face value (value at maturity). The computed interest on zeros accrues at a rate that will make them worth their face value at maturity.

One reason people like them is the enormous leverage potential. A slight drop in interest rates can send zeros soaring in price. They're a great way to speculate on lower interest rates.

But you should always consider the risks in buying zeros. First, a rise in interest rates can mean big losses. Second, consider the tax consequences. Even though you don't receive regular interest payments on zeros, the IRS taxes you on the *phantom interest*, as if you had received it regularly.

For this reason, many people who hold their zeros to maturity either put them into a tax-deferred retirement account, such as an IRA or Keogh Plan, or put them in a child's name to fund his or her education.

Finally, the cost of buying zeros can be horrendous. Commissions and markups on zero-coupon bonds are sometimes much higher than they are on other bonds. The North American Securities Administrators Association and the Council of Better Business Bureaus issued an alert several years ago saying that some brokers were charging a markup as high as 15% on zero-coupon bonds. It's imperative that you shop around before buying such bonds.

As a low-cost alternative, invest in a zero-coupon bond fund. The best series is the Benham Target Maturity Trust series, available from Benham Capital Management (800/4-SAFETY or 415/965-4274). These are all no-load funds with reasonable management fees. A wide range of maturities is available on their zero-coupon bonds. Those with the longest maturities have the greatest profit potential . . . and the greatest risk.

$ COST-CUTTING TIP #37
Buy Bonds at $0.10 on the $1.00!

One interesting speculation is to buy the bonds of bankrupt companies—you can sometimes get them at pennies on the dollar. When Chrysler hovered near bankruptcy in the 1970s, the market value of its bonds plummeted. People who bought Chrysler bonds back then made huge profits, as Chrysler turned around in the 1980s. A similar situation happened with the Washington Public Power Supply bonds. Of course, the risk is that the company will default on everything, including the bonds.

If you're betting on a company to turn around after a bankruptcy, you're better off buying the company's bonds than its stock. Bonds are a company's senior security. They are backed by collateral, usually cash or equipment, which is pledged to be sold if the issuer defaults on an interest or principal payment. Generally, only bank loans or indebtedness are higher in priority for payment of interest or principal.

CHAPTER 6

Penny-Pinching on Penny Stocks

Patience in a market is worth pounds in a year.

—Ben Franklin

You wouldn't think that a penny stock would be so costly. But investors routinely overpay, sometimes by as much as 40%, on penny and OTC stocks—and usually, they never know it. Just because a stock sells for under $5 a share, which is now the standard definition of a *penny stock*, doesn't mean it's a bargain.

Of course, some penny stocks—if bought wisely—can be tremendous bargains, and Uncle Scrooge is always interested in a bargain! Some of these small companies might have big profit potential. It isn't unusual to find penny stocks trading at substantial discounts from their *intrinsic*, or breakup, value, and trading at ridiculously low P/E multiples of four or five.

The reason: These firms exist in an inefficient market that is largely overlooked by the Wall Street establishment. The institutions and major brokerage firms ignore them. So do the national financial media—*Money* magazine, *Business Week*, *Forbes*, and the *Wall Street Journal*.

But the opportunities exist. You have much greater leverage with penny stocks than you do with most of the stocks trading on the NYSE, the AMEX, or the upper tier of the OTC market. It would be far easier to double your money in a stock selling for $0.50 to $1.00, than it would be to double your money with IBM.

And just because a stock sells for a low price doesn't mean it's a small, insignificant company. Shares in the Hong Kong & Shanghai Bank regularly sell for less than $1 a share, yet it is one of the largest, most profitable banks in the world.

$ COST-CUTTING TIP #38
Guard Against Excessive Markups

As we've seen with bonds, the commission isn't the only way your stockbroker makes money. In penny stocks and other OTC transactions, an aggressive broker can make a fortune, either by marking the stock up when you buy or marking it down when you sell. In fact, your broker may even try to trick you into thinking you're getting the transaction for free by telling you there is no commission. Indeed, your trade confirmation and client statement will bear this out. But what it won't reveal is the huge profit the broker made on the *spread* (markup)—the difference between the bid price and the ask price.

Here's how a stock is marked up: A $2.50 stock might be marked up three-quarters of a point to $3.25. When sold, it might be marked down one-quarter of a point ($0.25) to $2.25. It may not sound like much, but 1,000 shares, at one-quarter of a point, is $250.00. Multiply that by the thousands of shares sold, and you can see how profitable it can be for some brokers. It's a good idea never to pay more than 20% over the *market maker*'s bid price. (The market maker is a brokerage firm that holds the stock in its own account.) If your broker is not a market maker, then he or she would go to the market maker to obtain the shares to sell to you.

$ COST-CUTTING TIP #39
Instruct Your Broker To Act
as Agent, Not Principal

If you ask the broker to act as your agent, he or she must give you the best available price at the time and fully disclose the commission on the order. Always ask your penny-stock broker to act as agent, rather than principal. If he or she refuses, either go elsewhere or try to find out the spread and negotiate it down.

$ COST-CUTTING TIP #40
Compare Price Quotes

It usually pays to compare price quotes from brokers. You could, for example, call several brokers, one right after the other, and buy from the one with the lowest quote. (This may not endear you to your broker.) If you trade penny stocks, you might open an account with Kennedy, Cabot & Co.—the discount broker that had the lowest fee for penny stocks of all the brokers I surveyed ($0.015 per share, $35.00 minimum, or $0.01 per share for 20,000 or more shares). Then, compare Kennedy's quote with the one your full-service broker gave you.

One of my recommended brokers, Rick Rule, charges a low commission (3.5%) for both low-price and foreign stocks, subject to a $60 minimum. You can reach him at Torrey Pines Securities, 140 Marine View Dr., Suite 110, Solana Beach, CA 92075, 800/356-8973 or 619/259-9921.

$ COST-CUTTING TIP #41
Don't Buy Right after a Newsletter Recommendation

Most penny stocks are thinly traded, with perhaps a few thousand shares changing hands daily. If a penny stock is recommended in a popular newsletter, it can send the price soaring. You're better off waiting two or three months, until the buying frenzy has died down and the stock's price has settled back to more reasonable levels.

Don't buy a penny stock if it has already risen several hundred percentage points. Chances are you'll be getting in at or near the top of the market.

$ COST-CUTTING TIP #42
Beware of Broker-Hyped Stocks

If a broker calls you with a hot stock, you should hang up. No matter how exciting the deal sounds, no matter how glib the presentation, never invest solely on the sales pitch of a broker—particularly one you hardly know and have never dealt with.

$ COST-CUTTING TIPS #43
Ten Pointers on Penny-Stock Buying

Following is a penny-stock checklist:

1. Always scrutinize the annual report and any other literature you can obtain about a small firm, including brokerage company reports. Brokers are sometimes prone to, shall we say, exaggeration. Written information is more accountable to regulation and may put the investment in a more realistic light. Pay close attention to the footnotes and fine print.
2. Stay away from companies with excessive debt or companies that are in bankruptcy.
3. Stay away from companies whose annual reports reveal too much of their assets under *goodwill* or that have negative working capital, poor earnings or significant legal problems.
4. Stay away from penny stocks with high *market capitalization*. (The market capitalization is the market value of a public company, determined by multiplying the number of issued shares by the trading price.)
5. Look for liquidity. A stock should trade at least 50,000 shares a week.
6. Diversify your penny-stock portfolio. You should be invested in at least six companies.
7. Ask brokers if they personally have a position in the stock

they're recommending. (It's best if they don't.) If so, ask if they have sold or are planning to sell any, or whether they purchased the stock at a price below the current offer.

8. Always take possession of penny-stock certificates.

9. In mining stocks, stick with firms that are in production or near it. Do not buy mining stocks in the earlier phases of growth—exploration, developmental exploration or development. It's difficult even for professional geologists and mining-stock experts to assess the future prospects of these.

10. Don't bet more than you can afford to lose. Penny stocks are speculative. Even if you've done your homework, you'll still probably lose your money. Take a flyer on them only if that doesn't bother you.

CHAPTER 7

Saving Money on Silver and Gold

All that glitters is not gold.

—WILLIAM SHAKESPEARE

I<small>F THERE</small> was one type of investment that was most precious to Uncle Scrooge, it was gold and silver. He loved his bags of old coins in the money bin. He used to bathe in it! It reminded him of his roots as a gold prospector. He also kept three cubic acres of gold and silver because he knew they were the only real money. Like Uncle Scrooge, I recommend you keep a few bags of coins around.

How to buy? Unfortunately, precious metals investors are routinely overcharged, which is surprising considering how easy it is to save money.

$ COST-CUTTING TIP #44
Choose from Six Low-Priced Dealers

For years, *Silver & Gold Report* (P.O. Box 2923, West Palm Beach, FL 33402) has anonymously surveyed some 25 of the country's precious metals dealers to see which ones have the lowest prices.

The savings can be tremendous. The surveys regularly show price differences of well over $1,000 for investments like 1,000 one-ounce silver Canadian Maple Leafs or 20 one-ounce gold coins, like South African Krugerrands. Simply by taking a few minutes to shop around, you can save hundreds, if not thousands, of dollars.

I've been following this survey for several years, and there are a handful of dealers that consistently seem to have the lowest prices in most categories. They are:

- Benham Certified Metals, 1665 Charleston Rd., Mountain View, CA 94043, 800/447-4653, in Alaska and Hawaii, 415/965-4275.
- Camino Coin, 875 Mahler Rd., Suite 150, Burlingame, CA 94010, 800/348-8001 or 415/348-3000.
- Dillon Gage, Inc., 15301 Dallas Pkwy., Suite 200, Dallas, TX 75248, 800/537-2583 or 214/788-4765.
- Rhyne Precious Metals, 425 Pike St., Suite 403, Seattle, WA 98101, 800/426-7835 or 206/623-6900.
- Sam Sloat, Inc., P.O. Box 192, 136 Main St., Westport, CT 06881, 800/243-5670 or 203/226-4279.
- SilverTowne, P.O. Box 424, Route 4, Old Union City Pike, Winchester, IN 47394, 800/788-7481 or 317/584-7481.

$ COST-CUTTING TIP #45
Comparison Shop

Unfortunately, it isn't wise to pick just one coin company and buy from it. You should call at least three companies, and preferably all six, one right after the other, to get quotes. Also, a coin dealer may have a low price for one item and a high price for another.

Always ask for the total amount, including all charges, you would have to send, rather than just getting per-ounce, per-bag, per-bar or per-coin quotes. Otherwise, some dealers may give you a low quote and then tack on all sorts of other charges for commissions, shipping, insurance, etc.

$ COST-CUTTING TIP #46
Buy the Lowest-Premium Gold Coins

If you're investing in gold bullion, you'll get the most for your money by buying either Austrian Coronas or South African Krugerrands. These generally sell for 1% over the spot price, while the other, more popular gold coins may sell at a premium of 5% or more. Surprisingly, Coronas and Krugerrands are even a better deal than gold bars.

$ COST-CUTTING TIP #47
Buy One-Ounce Gold Coins, Not Fractional Ones

Gold bullion coins are minted in sizes ranging from over one ounce to one-tenth ounce. You'll get significantly more gold for your money if you prefer the one-ounce coins to the fractional ounce.

Two one-half ounce gold coins will generally cost about 3.5% to 5% more than a one-ounce gold coin. Four one-quarter ounce gold coins are generally 6% to 9% more expensive than a one-ounce coin. Ten one-tenth-ounce gold coins are 10% to 22% more expensive than the one ounce.

$ COST-CUTTING TIP #48
Take Delivery in States with No Sales Tax on Coins and Bullion

Sales tax on coins and bullion varies from state to state, from zero to 10%, including local and county taxes. You can usually escape the tax entirely by purchasing coins from out of state, although there are increasing efforts by state tax authorities to force mail-order firms to charge individual state sales taxes. Already, major brokerage houses will charge you state sales tax if you take delivery of coin purchases.

FIGURE 7.1
The Best States in Which To Buy Coins and Precious Metals

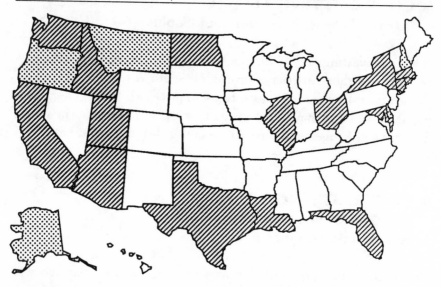

| | No state sales tax on some precious metals and coins | | No state sales tax |

State	Sales Tax on Precious Metals	State	Sales Tax on Precious Metals
Alaska	No state sales tax	Massachusetts	5% on sales of less than $1,000
Arizona	No tax on coins or bullion; 5% when in jewelry or art	Montana	No state sales tax
		New Hampshire	No state sales tax
California	No sales tax on gold or silver over $1,000	New York	4% on sales of less than $1,000; no tax on collector coins
Colorado	3% tax on all precious metals		
Connecticut	7.5% on sales of less than $1,000	North Carolina	3% tax on all precious metals
Delaware	No state sales tax	North Dakota	No tax on coins; 5% on bullion
Florida	No state sales tax on legal tender coins of any nation; 5% on other precious metals	Ohio	No tax on any coins or bullion
		Oregon	No state sales tax
Georgia	3% tax on all precious metals	Rhode Island	No tax on any coins or bullion
Idaho	No tax on coins or bullion; 5% when used in jewelry and art	Texas	4.125% on sales of less than $1,000
Illinois	5% on Krugerrands; all other coin and bullion sales exempt	Utah	No tax on coins or bullion
		Washington	No tax on any coins or bullion
Louisiana	4% on sales of less than $1,000	Wyoming	3% tax on all precious metals
Maryland	5% on sales of less than $1,000 for bullion and coins		

NOTE: County and city taxes may be additional.
SOURCE: Industry Council for Tangible Assets.

(However, coin purchases are exempt if you let the broker hold the coins for you.)

Generally, I don't recommend buying coins from brokerage houses because you lose privacy—they demand your social security number even when you *buy* (it's only required by law when you *sell*). And, they usually won't take cash.

If you want maximum privacy and lowest cost per coin, I recommend shopping around locally in a state that exempts coins from the sales tax. Surprisingly, about half of all states now exempt all or almost all coin sales, and the list is growing. Exemption is becoming popular because these states know that they are losing business to mail-order firms in other states that do not charge sales taxes. (See fig. 7.1.)

For the private investor, buying gold and silver in person at a local coin dealer is the best way to go. Just walk into the coin shop, select your investment, pay with cash and walk out the door. No name or social security number is recorded. However, I recommend that you get a receipt for tax purposes, in case you sell later.

$ COST-CUTTING TIP #49
The Cheapest Way To Buy Precious Metals

The cheapest way to buy precious metals is to go to a commodities broker, buy a futures contract for the nearest delivery date and take delivery. For a nominal fee, your precious metals will be stored for you in a safe, secure exchange-approved warehouse. Just remember, the minimum purchases are high. Table 7.1 lists the minimums, depending on the exchange:

TABLE 7.1
Precious Metal Purchases

Metal	Exchange	Minimum Purchase
Gold	Chicago Board of Trade	1 kilo (32.15 troy ounce)
Gold	COMEX	100 troy ounce
Silver	Chicago Board of Trade	1,000 troy ounce
Silver	COMEX	1,000 troy ounce
Silver	COMEX	5,000 troy ounce
Silver	Mid-America	1,000 troy ounce
Platinum	New York Mercantile	50 troy ounce
Palladium	New York Mercantile	100 troy ounce

CHAPTER 8

Cutting Your Fees on Commodity Futures

No profession requires more hard work, intelligence, patience, and mental discipline than successful speculating.

—ROBERT RHEA

WHEN TRADING commodities, commissions and fees can be real profit killers—more so than perhaps any other investment. Although many stock investors may only trade three or four times a year, commodity traders may have that many trades—or more—in a week or even a day.

Commissions at the full-service firms are high—$75 to $130 per contract. *Churning*—excessive trading by brokers to generate commissions—is sometimes a problem.

Even if you have an honest broker and know what you're doing, you can still lose your shirt. That's because of the powerful impact of leverage. For as little as $5,000 (the minimum account size at many firms), you can control a $50,000 to $100,000 contract. Your profit potential is magnified 10 to 20 times. But remember, just as your profits are leveraged, so are your losses. A slight move against you could wipe you out.

Commodity trading should almost always be considered speculative. If you must do it, I recommend that, at the very least, you educate yourself. Two excellent beginning books on commodity trading are *Getting Started in Futures* by Todd Lofton (New York: John Wiley & Sons, 1989) and *Facts on Futures* by Jake Bernstein (Chicago: Probus Publishing Co., 1987).

Free Info on Futures

You can get free information on the major commodity exchanges from the Commodity Futures Trading Commission (CFTC), 2033 K St., NW, Washington, D.C. 20581, 202/254-8630. Ask for the consumer affairs booklets on the basic commodity contracts, markets and regulations.

You can check out any commodity fund through the National Futures Association (NFA) (800/621-3570, in Illinois, 800/572-9400), a self-regulatory organization. It can verify whether or not a commodity fund operator is properly registered and if any disciplinary action has been taken against the pool operator. The NFA offers useful booklets and other information on trading commodities.

$ COST-CUTTING TIP #50
Use Low-Fee Commodity Funds

Most people are better off investing in commodities through a professional manager. But make sure you're paying a reasonable fee. Commodity funds are notorious for charging outrageous fees and commissions—up to 20% annually.

Here are three of the lowest-cost commodity funds in the country. At the time we went to press, all three were still open to new investors. But there's no guarantee that they will be by the time you read this book. There's also no guarantee that you'll make money in them, although one of them—Futures-1000 Plus—does guarantee that you'll get back your original investment over the five-year life of the program.

- Alternative Asset Growth Fund, structured as a limited partnership, is designed by commodity expert Gary D. Halbert, president, ProFutures, Inc. Based on detailed studies of the top-100 commodity futures managers, ProFutures selects the top-5 commodity managers and divides the fund's assets between them. The fund is diversified into stock, bond, currency, precious metals, oil, grains and other futures. You are guaranteed no margin calls, and you can take your money out at any month-ending date. You will also receive a free monthly newsletter updating the value of your fund. The fund, first offered in March 1990, was up 18% in its first year. And a new fund opened September 1991. Call for details.

  Contact: Gary Halbert, President, ProFutures, Inc., 107 Hwy. 620 South, Suite 30F, Austin, TX 78734, 800/348-3601 or 512/263-3800, fax: 512/263-3459. Minimum investment: $10,000.
- Timing Device Fund I, a fund created by commodity trader Kelly Angle, became available in October 1990. Angle was picked as having the highest rate of return combined with the smallest amount of dollars lost, in both 1989 and 1990, by *Commodity Traders Consumer Report*, an independent rating service. His fund has gotten off to a slow start, but given his track record, and the fund's low costs, it's worth considering.

  It has no front-end load, a *round-turn commission* (initiating and liquidating a position) of $15.20 (compared to $50.00 to $60.00 for some public futures funds), a 6% total annual management fee and a 15% quarterly incentive fee on new closed profits (and excluding any interest income). The fund follows a conservative strategy, with 80% of investors' funds earning a T-bill yield. The trading approach is to rank all the major futures markets and indices according to volatility and then trade only the 25% most active that are at the top of this volatility index.

For more information, contact: Kelly Angle & Co., 1020 East English, Wichita, KS 67211, 316/685-6034.

• The Shearson Futures-1000 Plus Series of funds, composed of 65% zero-coupon bonds and 35% commodity futures, contains some of my favorite commodity funds. Almost all previous recommendations (six out of seven) in the series have done superbly. What's more, they carry no long-term risk--if you hold for five years, you're assured of getting back your original investment.

How do they do it? When the fund starts investing, the managers put away 65% of the initial capital in zero-coupon bonds, which mature in five years at 100% of your original investment value. Then, they invest the remaining 35% in the commodity market. Many other major brokerage firms now have these *assured-return commodity funds*, but I like the Shearson plans best for their relatively low annual cost of 12.7% (others charge up to 20%).

For more information, call or write: Martin Truax, Shearson Lehman Brothers, 400 Perimeter Center Terrace NE, Suite 290, Atlanta, GA 30346, 800/241-6900, in Georgia, 800/282-5909.

$ COST-CUTTING TIP #51
Use Discount Commodity Brokers

If you want to go it alone in commodities, you might consider discount commodity brokers. Like discount stockbrokers, these firms won't give you any advice or hold your hand through the scary parts. But they will give you fast, efficient and courteous service and executions of your trades.

Table 8.1 compares the commission charges of the major commodity discount brokers.

TABLE 8.1

Comparison Survey: Major Commodity Discounters

Firm (Phone)	Intraday Trade	Overnight Trade	Options	Min. Acct.
First American (800/621-4415, 312/368-4700)	$25	$25	$25	$5,000
Futures Discount Group (800/872-6673, 312/444-1155)	26	26	29	5,000
Ira Epstein & Co. (800/284-6000, 312/207-1800)	24	29	35	5,000
Jack Carl (800/621-3424, 312/407-5700)	25	30	35	5,000
TransMarket Group (800/362-8117, 312/663-4972)	27	29	35	5,000

All the above prices are for full-size contracts, based on round turns. Different commissions may apply if you trade smaller contracts on the Mid-America exchange. If you're doing sophisticated strategies—like spreads, combinations, butterflies or boxes—you should check to see what the commissions are. Many firms also charge extra for exchange fees, which run $1 to $3 per contract. Some firms also offer free charts, newsletters and hotlines.

You must be cautious in choosing a futures broker because there is no government insurance to protect your funds should the firm go under. Make sure the firm you choose has been in business for at least five years—and preferably longer. All of the above firms listed in table 8.1 meet this criterion.

When dealing with a commodities broker, you'll want to make sure that any profits you make, above and beyond the margin requirements, are held in a segregated money market account. That way, you'll be protected if the company collapses. Also, make sure that all the cash in your account is earning interest at a competitive rate.

$ COST-CUTTING TIP #52
Never Meet a Margin Call

This is standard advice from many commodity trading experts, but it bears repeating. A margin call occurs when the market moves against you so severely that the broker sends you a formal demand for money, first by phone, and then followed by telex, fax or telegram. If you don't meet it immediately, by wiring funds, your position is liquidated.

Meeting margin calls can eat up a tremendous amount of money. If you get a margin call, it's usually a clear sign that you have called the market wrong. By meeting it, you're throwing good money after bad. Your losses could keep mounting. Liquidating your position on the first margin call will assure that you'll limit your losses in commodity trading.

$ COST-CUTTING TIP #53
Treat Some Commodities as Long-Term Investments

Some of my good friends in the newsletter business—notably Doug Casey, editor of *Crisis Investing,* and John Pugsley, editor of *John Pugsley's Journal*—advocate a strategy of using commodities as long-term, buy-and-hold investments rather than as trading vehicles. This strategy saves enormously in transaction costs, yet still retains some of the leveraged profit potential. Here's how it works:

You buy the futures contract with the furthest delivery month possible—which can be as long as two years with some contracts. You put up 50% or more, rather than the 5% or 10% that most commodity traders put up, to protect yourself against wide swings in the price. Then, you simply sit on the contract and wait for the price to rise. Meanwhile, you earn interest at the T-bill rate on your deposit. If it doesn't rise by the delivery month, you simply roll it over. This strategy works best if you buy when a commodity is near its historically low levels, when it is selling below its cost of production or when you feel certain its price has bottomed out.

CHAPTER 9

Big Savings When You Buy Real Estate

You may buy land now as cheap as stinking mackerel.

—WILLIAM SHAKESPEARE

YOU CAN cut your costs tremendously when you buy real estate. At every stage—from finding the property to closing the deal—there are opportunities to save money. Scratch beneath the surface of any successful real estate investor, and you'll find a real Scrooge.

$ COST-CUTTING TIP #54
Advice from John Schaub on Buying Right

One of my favorite real estate experts is John Schaub—a man who truly knows how to be a skinflint. He has survived and prospered in the booms and busts in real estate over the last 20 years because he is so careful in risk management. He buys only 1 out of 100 homes or properties he examines. Here are some of his tips on buying right:

- Before you start, make a list of exactly what you want in a property.
- Become well versed in the market by systematically examining properties, talking to sellers and making offers. You might also

hire appraisers. They're usually well worth the $100 or so they charge.

- Deal directly with the owner rather than an agent or employee. The owner knows better than anyone what the bottom price will be. If you're looking at ads in the newspaper, concentrate on the For Sale by Owner ads.
- Find someone who is anxious to sell. You might, for example, read the obituaries to find the representative of an estate to see if the deceased's house will be sold. Loan companies might tell you about people who are behind on their loans. Check the public records to see who has filed for divorce. As you drive through prospective neighborhoods, look for houses that look as though no one lives in them.
- Before you make an offer, always find out, from the public record, what sellers paid for the property and how long they owned it.
- Always make an offer. Even if it's refused, you learn something about how people react. The more offers you make, the better you'll be at it.
- When you meet better negotiators, study their techniques, but don't try to outsmart them.
- Remember the 10-10-10 guidelines. Buy at a price at least 10% below the market value. Pay a maximum interest rate of 10%. Negotiate hard on interest and drive it as low as possible. Make a maximum down payment of 10%.

Schaub and other real estate experts are also recommending that you take full advantage of *distress sales*, which appear to be a growth industry in the 1990s—foreclosures are big business. Be on the lookout for super bargains, sometimes 30% or more below the appraised market, from banks, the IRS, VA or RTC. The Resolution Trust Corporation, set up by Congress to bail out the savings and loan industry, is offering thousands of properties at bargain prices. Contact their offices in major cities throughout the country.

If you're planning to buy real estate, I strongly urge you to get a copy of Schaub's book *Buying Right* and subscribe to his newsletter. You can order the book from ProServe, 1938 Ringling Blvd., Sarasota, FL

34236, 800/237-9222 (includes Canada) or 813/366-9024. The price is $16.95. He doesn't usually send out free sample copies of his newsletter, *John Schaub's Strategies & Solutions*, but mention this book, and he'll send you one.

$ COST-CUTTING TIP #55
Shop for the Best Mortgage

When looking for a mortgage, it pays to call several lenders and compare rates. Don't just go with your broker's recommendation. Figure out how much you will pay each month for each scenario. For adjustable rate mortgages, assume interest rates will rise the maximum allowed by law. Read all mortgage documents carefully. Make sure they don't contain a lot of restrictive clauses or add-on charges. Some, for example, may require that you pay the bank's attorney's fees and processing expenses. Negotiate to have these removed.

One useful resource is the Home Buyer's Mortgage Kit. Included in the kit is a listing of the mortgage rates and terms available in any 1 of 36 major metropolitan areas around the country. It's an easy way to compare rates among various mortgage lenders. Also included is *How to Shop for Your Mortgage*, a 44-page booklet designed to educate homeowners about the mortgage market. The cost for the kit is $20. For information or to order, contact: HSH Associates, 1200 Route 23 North, Butler, NJ 07405, 800/UPDATES or 201/838-3330.

$ COST-CUTTING TIP #56
Save Big Money on Closing
Costs and Commissions

The best way to save on closing costs is to avoid dealing with banks and mortgage companies altogether. Use Schaub's technique of financing directly with sellers. You'll avoid all the costs associated with a bank loan—a second appraisal, mortgage title insurance, etc. If you're an

experienced investor, you can also save money by not having properties appraised.

And here's a little-known way to eliminate the 6% sales commission
and reduce closing costs when selling a house: Lease your property
with an option to buy!

Here's how a lease option works: Suppose you want to sell a rental
house appraised for $115,000. You place a classified ad in the local
paper, "Rent with option to buy." You offer to rent the place for $900 a
month, higher than the market rent. The rental income consists of
$700 rent and a $200 option fee. The option permits the tenants to buy
the property for $115,000 at any time during the ensuing year. Set a
price that the tenants will find attractive. It has to be a good deal for
both parties or a lease option won't work.

The option agreement states that the monthly option fee can be
used toward a down payment on the house. If the tenant decides not to
buy the house after a year, he or she may forfeit all or part of the option
fee, depending on the contract agreement.

Here are the benefits of a lease option:

- You get an additional $200 a month in income, part or all of which
  you get to keep if the tenant does not exercise the option.
- Option fees are not taxable to you until the option is exercised or
  abandoned.
- You avoid the 6% real estate agent's commission when you sell the
  house. This is a potential savings of $7,000 in our example.
- Even if the option is not exercised, your property is likely to be
  better maintained. Renters with a lease option take better care of
  their future home.
- Lease options usually make it easier to rent your house. More
  people are likely to respond to your ad because it will attract
  people who want to buy a house but lack a sufficient down payment right now. They may have the down payment in a year but
  not now. And they may need the forced savings of a monthly
  option plan.

Schaub has a special report on lease options, which contains sample
contracts and all the details. Send $15 to ProServe to obtain a copy.

$ COST-CUTTING TIP #57
A No-Load Fund for Undervalued Real Estate

Do you want to invest in undervalued real estate but not hunt for properties, negotiate deals and perform the countless other necessary tasks? A colleague at Phillips Publishing, Peter Dickinson, editor of *The Retirement Letter*, recommends T. Rowe Price's Renaissance Fund.

The fund specializes in *undervalued real estate*, quality real estate at low prices. Most are commercial properties located in Dallas, Denver and parts of Florida. This isn't for those looking for income from a real estate investment but for those looking for capital gains, when these markets complete their turnaround, some years down the road.

For more information, contact: T. Rowe Price Investor Services, 100 East Pratt St., Baltimore, MD 21202, 800/322-5869 or 301/547-2308.

$ COST-CUTTING TIP #58
Buy Mortgages at a Discount
and Earn 15% or More!

One great income-producing investment is the discounted mortgage market, which offers several advantages over real estate—including better liquidity, better cash flow, no management responsibilities and rates of return of over 20% if you shop carefully.

On the downside, there are no tax breaks, and you can't profit from the property's appreciation unless the owner defaults—and default is a danger. You may end up with a piece of property that has no value.

Here's how discounted mortgages work: Many sellers of real estate have taken back second mortgages in order to close the deal. A large number of holders of second mortgages would like to sell them before they mature because: (a) they need more money sooner, (b) they have income tax problems or (c) they fear they won't get paid, especially if balloon payments are involved.

For these and other reasons, many such people will sell their seconds at a substantial discount. For example, a $10,000, five-year note at 12% interest means the seller is getting $222 a month. Suppose four years are left on the second, and the seller wants out. The balance due after one year is $8,450. If you purchased the second for approximately $7,800, which sounds like a reasonable offer, you would earn 20% on your money.

Where do you find second mortgages?

- Contact several real estate brokers in the area and let them know you are willing to buy seconds.
- Go to your local county deed office and get the names of individuals who have seconds on properties.
- Place classified ads in the local newspaper saying, "Private party has cash to buy existing notes and mortgages."

Following are some important caveats:

- Before buying seconds, check out the financial condition of the property owners, especially their main source of income.
- Stay away from mortgages with large balloon payments, which are seldom paid off on time and must be renegotiated.
- Make sure there is lots of equity in the property.
- If the owner defaults on your second, he or she may default on the first mortgage as well. In order to collect your money, you must continue paying the first mortgage while you foreclose the house! Otherwise, you'll likely end up with nothing.
- Avoid leveraging debt (i.e., don't borrow money from a bank to buy a note).
- Don't tell the owner of the property that you are buying the note at a discount; he or she may want to pay it off to save money.
- Finally, beware of closing costs, such as title insurance and recording your second at the courthouse. Closing costs can reduce your real return significantly.

Obviously, I've only scratched the surface with this thumbnail introduction to discount mortgage investing. Real estate expert Schaub has an excellent six-hour tape series called *Investing in Paper*, which covers investing in first and second mortgages, and includes a 65-page workbook. You can order the book from ProServe. The cost is $149. You will also get a free copy of Jim Napier's book *Invest in Debt: The "How to" Book on Buying Paper for Cash Flow.* Separately, it's $12.

CHAPTER 10

Cutting Costs on Rare Coins, Collectibles and Antiques

Beware of little expenses. A small leak will sink a great ship.

—Ben Franklin

Perhaps nowhere is there more overcharging than in collectibles. Why? Because most buyers don't know value. The main reason dealers can charge high markups is because the customers willingly pay them, without doing their homework.

$ COST-CUTTING TIP #59
Learn To Evaluate the Condition of the Collectibles You're Buying

As one collectibles expert says, "Just as in real estate, the magic word is location, location, location, so in collectibles, it is condition, condition, condition. Collectors in some fields are absolute fanatics about condition.

"For instance," he adds, "comic book people are amazingly stringent in their requirements. If that staple has a tiny bit of rust on it, that can downgrade your book. Sheet music people are the same way. They don't want a cat hair, they don't want a tear, they don't want your name written in the upper corner."

The best way to learn value is to attend auctions, visit shops, ask questions of the experts and read everything you can find about the particular collectibles you're interested in. The public library is a great place to start.

$ COST-CUTTING TIP #60
Know the Value of the Collectibles You're Buying

You need to know not only how to evaluate the condition of an item, but also what price to pay for it. An almost microscopic scratch on a rare coin, for example, could cut the value by more than half. A particular carnival glass vase could sell for anywhere from $30 to $800, depending on its color. That's how finicky some collectors are.

Again, you can learn something about value by shopping around and asking questions. Some excellent price guides are also available.

One good general price guide is the *Antique Trader's Price Guide* (P.O. Box 1050, Dubuque, IA 52004, 319/588-2073, $13.50 per year, $2.95 per copy). Each specialty, if large enough, may have its own price guides. In rare coins, for example, the best guides are the *Coin Dealer Newsletter* (*CDN*) for wholesale raw coins and the *Certified Coin Dealer Newsletter* (*CCDN*) for coins that have been graded through a grading service—PCGF, NGC, NCI or ANACS (P.O. Box 11099, Torrance, CA 90510). Published weekly, these newsletters give the recent wholesale prices of the most widely traded U.S. rare coins. Subscription prices for *CDN* are $50 for six months and $89 a year; for *CCDN*, it's $56 and $99, respectively.

$ COST-CUTTING TIP #61
Comparison Shop Between Galleries and Dealers

It's hard to shop for collectibles because each one is different. It's like comparing apples and kumquats in many cases. That's where having expertise comes in handy.

Another problem is finding dealers who handle the items you're interested in. If you collect alpaca sweaters, you might find that the dealers for such an esoteric item are spread far and wide. With more common items, such as U.S. rare coins or stamps, comparison shopping is considerably easier, although it still suffers from the handicap that no two coins or stamps are exactly alike.

An excellent sourcebook, which cross-indexes dealers and collectors according to their specialties, is *I'll Buy That* (recently updated). It's a good place to find all the major dealers in a particular item. The book is available from Treasure Hunt Publications, P.O. Box 3028, Pismo Beach, CA 93449, 805/773-6777. The price is $23.95 postpaid.

One area where you can save a lot of money in comparison shopping is in *fine prints of famous artists*. Limited prints, often signed by the artist, have become an affordable way to profit from the art explosion. Original paintings and drawings from famous artists sell for millions. Only the superrich can now afford to buy them. Limited-edition signed prints are a viable alternative for private investors who want to create a nice collection. Only a few hundred lithographs, etchings or silk screen prints are made, and then the plates are destroyed. The artist signs the prints, which are then sold to the public.

Limited-edition signed prints have also skyrocketed in price, but you don't have to pay retail. You can save around 30% by avoiding the high-priced galleries in resorts and major cities and purchasing your prints by mail. Fine Arts Ltd. is a mail-order gallery specializing in limited-edition prints. The company has been in business since 1976. Founder Michael B. Kuschmann includes works by Renoir, Picasso, Erté, Rembrandt, Chagall, Delacroix and McKnight. Last year I wanted to buy a McKnight painting. Most of the galleries wanted about $1,400 for the print I was looking for. Fine Arts Ltd. sold it to me for $950.

Kuschmann also can act as a dealer for other types of art. One of my subscribers was just about to purchase an Erté bronze for full retail ($12,000). He called Fine Arts Ltd. and got it for $5,750. I recommend you contact Fine Arts Ltd. before you make any major purchase at a gallery.

For more information on saving money on art, contact Michael B.

Kuschmann, Director, Fine Arts Ltd., 220 State St., Suite H, Los Altos, CA 94022, 800/229-4322, 415/941-4322.

$ COST-CUTTING #62
Buy Through Auctions

Auctions can be a wonderful place to buy collectibles. Sometimes you can buy at auction cheaper than you can anywhere else. Many dealers do much of their buying at auctions. Here are a few tips:

- Attend specialized auctions of particular items rather than large, general auctions, where a wide variety of items are sold.
- Attend wholesale auctions, which have a large amount of dealers.
- Attend auctions where there is a need to sell (i.e., estate sales, bankruptcies and IRS auctions).
- Attend auctions where there is no minimum bid.
- Set price limits on each item you're bidding on, and don't go beyond your limit.

Auctions are usually advertised in the weekend section of major newspapers. You can also get on the mailing list of auctions in your area by calling up the auctioneers in the Yellow Pages and asking them to keep you informed of upcoming events.

The country's two leading auction houses are Sotheby's (1334 York Ave., New York, NY 10021, 800/444-3709 or 212/606-7000) and Christie's (502 Park Ave., New York, NY 10022, 718/784-1480); each offer dozens of catalogs every year. Subscriptions run from $15 to $800 a year, but if you're a serious auction buyer, they can be well worth it. Write or call both companies for a brochure describing their publications.

$ COST-CUTTING TIP #63
Don't Buy Manufactured Rarities

There may be a few exceptions, but, generally, limited-edition collector items, such as coins, plates and artwork, aren't even worth looking at. These are manufactured on assembly lines by professional direct marketing firms and sold at high prices.

They're usually not worth it. For most of these items, there isn't a large enough collector base to support the high prices, despite the claims of the advertisers. Wait a couple of years, and you'll be able to go to a secondhand store and buy the same piece for a fraction of the original offering price.

$ COST-CUTTING TIP #64
Don't Buy New Issues of Commemorative and Proof Coins

R. W. Bradford, editor of the coin newsletter *Analysis & Outlook*, wrote an article for the March 9, 1989, issue of *Barron's*, in which he showed that nearly all the coins sold by the U.S. Mint were terrible investments. A few issues, like one of the lower-mintage Olympic sets, did well. But over 90% of the new issues sold by the U.S. Mint have fallen below their initial offering price within a few years of their minting. I've found this to be true with many new issues of foreign commemorative coins as well.

You're better off avoiding all new commemorative and collector coins when they're first issued. If you want to own the coin, wait a year or two and buy it in the secondary market. Chances are, you'll pay a lot less for it.

▶*Free Sample:* Bradford publishes one of the better newsletters on the rare-coin market. Like me, he has a Scrooge mentality and is always trying to steer his readers away from the overpriced items and into the overlooked bargains. I've arranged for you to get a free sample copy of his newsletter, *R. W. Bradford's Analysis & Outlook*, P.O. Box 1167, Port Townsend, WA 98368. (It's regularly $78 a year for 12 issues.)

CHAPTER 11

Smart Shopping on Life Insurance Products

Nothing is certain in this life but death and taxes.

—BEN FRANKLIN

INSURANCE PROBABLY poses more problems for the cost-cutting investor than any other investment or consumer product. There are about 2,000 life insurance companies in the United States, some offering a multitude of policies. Hidden costs and undisclosed commissions abound.

Nevertheless, it is possible—and, once you know a few simple, Scrooge-like stratagems, surprisingly easy—to cut through the confusing jargon, the sales hype and the seemingly infinite variety of policies to shop smartly for insurance. In the process, you likely will save thousands of dollars.

$ COST-CUTTING TIP #65
Don't Buy Life Insurance
If You Don't Need It

It may seem silly even to suggest this, but every year, thousands of people buy life insurance they don't need. The purpose of life insurance, for most people, is to protect dependents in case of premature death.

Thus, most young, childless single people don't need life insurance. Neither do most married couples without children, especially if they both have careers. If they have children later, they can always buy it then. Neither do elderly people, whose children are grown and self-supporting, nor couples with several hundreds of thousands in financial assets.

$ COST-CUTTING TIP #66
Don't Buy More Insurance than You Need

Many people, when buying insurance, just pick an arbitrary figure—say $500,000. That's a mistake. You may end up buying more insurance than you really need. It's also a bad idea to follow blindly the insurance salesperson's advice on how much you need.

Here's how to determine the optimum amount of insurance. Add together funeral expenses, debts your heirs must pay and the income needs of your dependents. Subtract from these the resources your family will have to meet these expenses, such as bank accounts, stocks, bonds, mutual funds, marketable real estate, IRA/Keogh accounts, group life insurance, Social Security benefits and death benefits from pension plans.

If you have a large estate, make sure your heirs will have enough money to pay estate taxes without having to make a distressed sale of the estate's assets. You also need to figure on higher inflation.

$ COST-CUTTING TIP #67
Buy Term—the Least-Cost, Lowest-Commission Life Insurance

The standard advice often given about insurance is to "buy annual renewable term and invest the difference." Annual renewable term expires after one year, but you can renew the protection for one or more additional one-year periods without having to qualify for the insurance again.

With term, you get no accrual of cash value and no ability to borrow. You don't receive any money unless you die. But there are advantages: You generally get the most insurance for the least cost with term, as it generally carries much lower commissions. *Term insurance* is more cut and dried and easier to understand than *whole life*, the other major type of life insurance. Term insurance, however, doesn't have the tax benefits that whole life does. It can also become more expensive the older you get. Most cash-value policies maintain a stable premium throughout the life of the policy.

$ COST-CUTTING TIP #68
Should You "Buy Term and Invest the Difference"?

The standard advice for years is still excellent advice for many people. However, *cash-value life insurance*, on which money accrues over the life of the policy, offers some distinct advantages.

First, if you have trouble saving money, it forces you to save. Second, taxes are deferred on the increase in the cash value of your life insurance. Third, the money that you do invest is earning money, for both you and the insurance company. Fourth, you can borrow against the cash value of your policy, although the interest charged will be greater than the interest your money earned. Fifth, wealthy families (estates of over $600,000) can use life insurance to avoid estate taxes and pay probate expenses (state inheritance tax laws vary, so consult your attorney if you're interested in the details).

Thus, you should not ignore cash-value life insurance. Although the theory to "buy term and invest the difference" still works for many people—especially people in their twenties to forties, it may not necessarily be the best for you.

$ COST-CUTTING TIP #69
How To Get the Best Deal on Term Insurance

It's easy to compare policies for term insurance. Several companies will give you quotes from different insurers. All you do is call them and answer a few questions, like your age, whether or not you smoke and the amount of coverage you need. Within a week, you'll receive a printout containing information on several of the least-expensive, highly rated insurance companies. For information, call:

- Insurance Quote Services, Inc., 3200 North Dobson Rd., Bldg. C, Chandler, AZ 85224, 800/972-1104 or 602/345-7241, is run by David T. Phillips & Co., a pioneer in low-cost insurance shopping. They will send you a list of the five cheapest term policies from companies rated A+ by A. M. Best.
- Select Quote Insurance Services, 140 Second St., San Francisco, CA 94105, 800/343-1985 or 415/543-7338. They will send five quotes for each of two policy face amounts.
- Insurance Information, Inc., 23 Route 134, South Dennis, MA 02660, 800/472-5800 or 508/394-9117. Of the three, this is the only one that charges for quotes. The fee is $50, refundable if it can't find a policy cheaper than your current one. (This is strictly a referral service; it is the only one of the three that doesn't operate an insurance agency.)

Bear in mind that the cheapest first-year term policy is not necessarily the cheapest over a five- or ten-year period. Check the rates for each year.

$ COST-CUTTING TIP #70
Buy Low-Load and No-Load
Cash-Value Insurance

Your first choice in buying cash-value insurance is to stick with low-load and no-load policies. Low-load policies have commissions, but they're one-third to one-fourth the size of the commissions on most cash-value insurance. Some of these can be bought by mail, and you don't even have to deal with an insurance agent. Another advantage is that it costs you less to bail out of them—the surrender charges are more favorable on low-load insurance products.

Here are some companies that sell low-load and no-load life insurance:

- John Alden (800/874-5662)
- American Life, NY (212/581-1200)
- Ameritas (800/552-3553)
- Colonial Penn (800/874-5662)
- Fidelity Investments (800/343-2430)
- Lincoln Benefit (800/525-9287)
- USAA (800/531-8000)

Savings banks in Connecticut, Massachusetts and New York also sell low-load life insurance to residents of those states.

Just remember, if you're buying low-load insurance, it will take some research. If you have trouble making up your mind, you should look for other alternatives. Nevertheless, even if you are planning to buy through an insurance agent, it doesn't hurt to get quotes on low-load policies. You might be able to use these policies as ammunition to negotiate with insurance agents for the lower-commission policies their companies sell.

For more information on low-load life insurance, check out the *Individual Investor's Guide to Low-Load Life Insurance* by Glenn Daily. It's available in most bookstores, or you can order it from: Probus Publishing, 1925 North Clybourn St., Chicago, IL 60614, 800/776-2871 or 312/943-7354, $26.45, including postage and handling. Illinois residents add 8% sales tax.

For information on insurance companies that have low-commission products, some of which are sold directly and some of which are sold through brokers, contact: Council of Life Insurance Consultants, 600 W. Jackson, Room 800, Chicago, IL 60661, 800/533-0777 or 312/993-0355.

$ COST-CUTTING TIP #71
Use My Top-Two Recommended Insurance Agents

The insurance industry is changing every month, with new products and varying commissions. For over a decade, I've recommended two firms for the best deal for term, annuities whole life and variable products. I suggest you give them a call for your needs:

- David T. Phillips & Co., 3200 North Dobson Rd., Bldg. C, Chandler, AZ 85224, 800/223-9610 or 602/897-6088.
- Andrew D. Westhem, Western Capital Financial Group, 1925 Century Park East, Suite 2350, Los Angeles, CA 90067, 800/423-4891 or 213/556-5499.

$ COST-CUTTING TIP #72
The Lowest-Cost Variable Annuities

Right now, the two least-expensive variable-annuity products are:

- Vanguard's Variable Annuity. Annual fees for insurance and administration are approximately 1%, substantially lower than other annuities. It also has no up-front load or early withdrawal penalties. Choose between four funds, and switch at any time without penalty or tax consequence. Contact Vanguard, P.O. Box 2600, Valley Forge, PA 19482, 800/522-5555.
- Scudder's Horizon Plan. Annual fees are 1.5%, slightly higher than Vanguard's, but Scudder offers seven fund choices, including its international fund. Contact Scudder, 160 Federal St., Boston, MA 02110, 800/225-2470.

$ COST-CUTTING TIP #73
Four More Important Insurance
Shopping Pointers

Some further suggestions:

- Deal only with full-time agents who have been in the business for at least three years.
- Try to get testimonial letters from other clients.
- Ask the agents to disclose their commission.

No matter what kind of insurance you're buying, choose only a company that has an A-Plus rating in *Best's Insurance Reports*, which analyzes the financial strength of insurance companies, plus a stellar rating from *Standard & Poor's* (AA or above) or *Moody's*. These ratings are available in most public libraries. To be conservative, buy only from those companies that have an A-Plus rating from Best, plus a current top rating elsewhere.

$ COST-CUTTING TIP #74
How To Get a 50% Rebate on Commissions
for Insurance and Annuities

Insurance commission rebates are currently legal only in two states— California and Florida. But you don't necessarily have to live in either state to take advantage of them.

Insurance rebates work like this: Take a life insurance policy with a first-year premium of $10,000. The insurance company pays 70% of this premium, or $7,000, to the agency as a commission. But, with a 50% rebate, you can get back $3,500!

I recommend Jack White & Co., the California-based discount broker, as a source for these huge rebates on commissions. If your insurance purchase is large enough, it may be worthwhile to fly to California or Florida to sign the papers.

For more information on insurance rebating, contact: Jack White &

Co.'s insurance subsidiary, Direct Insurance Services, 9191 Towne
Centre Dr., Room 222, San Diego, CA 92122, 800/622-3699 or
619/552-2000. The firm offers rebates on whole life, annuities and
disability insurance.

$ COST-CUTTING TIP #75
Avoid Universal Life

Universal life is sometimes called *adjustable premium whole life*. I
don't recommend it. Although the cash value of universal life is more
readily available, you may reduce the death benefits if you withdraw it.
Also, early withdrawal—say before 15 years—may trigger tax consequences.

CHAPTER 12

Slashing Fees in Offshore Investments and Foreign Currencies

Merchants have no country.

—THOMAS JEFFERSON

INVESTING OFFSHORE presents its own particular problems to the cost-conscious investor. Some foreign banks charge high fees—higher than U.S. banks. Discount brokerage firms are almost nonexistent in foreign countries. No-load funds are not nearly as popular in foreign countries as they are in the United States. Yet, despite the difficulties, there are ways for you to cut costs when investing offshore.

$ COST-CUTTING TIP #76
How To Invest in Foreign Currencies— and Get the Bank Rate! (or Very Close to It)

If you buy currencies as investments, you probably pay 2% or 3% over the spot price. But, you can cut that charge to almost zero and, in fact, get the *bank rate*, the same rate that large institutions enjoy. The method is simple: Invest in foreign currencies through Shearson Lehman Brothers' no-load foreign currency funds.

Shearson offers five foreign currency funds—one is a managed basket of currencies and the other four are single-currency portfolios. They invest in short-term money market instruments from various countries. Being large buyers, they enjoy institutional rates for foreign currency purchases, typically 0.05%!

The four single-currency portfolios are an easy way to invest in the Canadian dollar, German deutsche mark, British pound sterling or Japanese yen. The total operating expense is a low 0.8%. Even with the management fee tacked on, this may be the lowest-cost method of investing in foreign currencies available. You can switch from these into some 30 other Shearson funds, but be careful because some of those other funds have high loads.

Because these are no-load funds, many Shearson brokers are not knowledgeable—or even aware—of them. Here are two that are: Ralph Goldman, Shearson Lehman Brothers, 120 N. 3rd St., Muskogee, OK 74401, 800/331-9757 or 918/683-5908; and Martin Truax, Shearson Lehman Brothers, 400 Perimeter Center Terrace, NE, Suite 290, Atlanta, GA 30346, 800/241-6900 or 404/393-2000.

$ COST-CUTTING TIP #77
How To Get the Best Rate on Foreign Currencies in Small Amounts or When You Travel

Depending on the currency, the location and the vendor, you could pay anywhere from 0.5% to 7% over the bank rate. The best way to get small amounts of foreign currency is to buy through banks, not currency dealers. You also get a better rate for traveler's checks than you do for cash.

You'll usually get a better exchange rate in the country in which the currency circulates than you will in a different country. For example, if you're buying British pounds, you'll get a better rate in London than you will in Paris, Amsterdam or New York. Use vacation trips to stock up on currencies.

$ COST-CUTTING TIP #78
Smart Shopping for Currencies

If you're buying currencies to send abroad, say, to open a bank account, purchase shares in an offshore fund or even to pay for hotel reservations, it pays to shop around.

1. Try your local banks—large commercial banks, particularly in big cities, often have a foreign-exchange department.
2. Get prices from several sources. Always ask for the total price. Say to them, "I need 10,000 Swiss francs [or whatever]. How much, in total, will those cost me?" Make sure there are no other charges.
3. Get prices from more than one dealer. Call several, one right after the other. Some sources for foreign currencies follow. All of them can accommodate anyone, anywhere in the country, whether you're buying cash, traveler's checks or wiring funds.

- American Automobile Association offers commission-free American Express traveler's checks to its members. Some AAA travel agencies also offer them commission free to their clients. They are offered in five currencies, and if you're buying in any currency but the U.S. dollar, you will pay a fee for the currency conversion. Check the White Pages of your telephone directory for the AAA office nearest you.
- Thomas Cook Inc. (formerly Deak International, 29 Broadway, New York, NY 10006, 212/757-6915) offers Thomas Cook traveler's checks in all major currencies at 110 branch offices throughout the United States. Call toll-free information (800/555-1212) or check your local Yellow Pages, under Foreign Exchange, for the office nearest you.
- Guardian International, Inc. (2499 North Harrison St., Arlington, VA 22207, 800/642-2208 or 703/237-1133, fax: 703/237-1883). Besides foreign currency traveler's checks (11 different types), the firm will also make electronic transfers of funds abroad.

- Mark Twain Bank (1630 South Lindbergh Blvd., St. Louis, MO 63131, 800/926-4922 or 314/997-9207) offers foreign exchange, electronic funds transfers and a variety of foreign currency CDs. However, it charges a 1% commission on its traveler's checks.
- Ruesch International (1350 Eye St., NW, 10th Fl., Washington, D.C. 20005, 800/424-2923 or 202/408-1200) sells Thomas Cook traveler's checks (at no commission), denominated in nine currencies, plus other foreign currency–related services. It charges a negligible $2 fee, regardless of the amount, for each currency.

$ COST-CUTTING TIP #79
How To Find the Lowest-Cost Foreign Bank

The best way to find the lowest-cost foreign bank is to determine what your needs are, and then find a bank that offers the best price for serving those needs. For example, if you deposit many small U.S. dollar checks, you would seek out a bank that had a reasonable fee for depositing U.S. dollar checks.

If you're looking for a bank as a place to provide safekeeping for your securities, you would seek out a bank that has low fees for that service. It may be that you'll want to use more than one bank, depending on what your needs are.

Small investors might be better off having only one or two accounts, while large investors might have as many as five accounts, depending on their needs. The following few tips describe some foreign banks that have a reputation for both excellent service and reasonable fees on certain services.

$ COST-CUTTING TIP #80
Try the Hong Kong & Shanghai Bank for a High-Interest, Low-Cost Savings Account

The Hong Kong & Shanghai Bank offers a high-yielding savings account in ten currencies. You can have a fixed account, ranging from

2 weeks to 12 months, and you can switch to any other currency, at any time, when the fixed period expires. You can add to or withdraw from your account at any time.

A service fee is charged only when you open or deposit money into the account. It charges 0.25%, plus HK$80 (about US$11) to deposit checks. The minimum investment is a low US$150, but I recommend you start with a minimum of $1,000 and preferably more. This is a far better deal than a deposit account with Swiss banks, which have not only much higher minimums but also a 35% withholding tax on interest.

The Hong Kong & Shanghai Bank is one of the world's largest, strongest banks. It is well diversified around the world, and it should remain stable even in the face of Red China's takeover of Hong Kong in 1997. For a free brochure on the Combinations Savings Account, write to: Hong Kong & Shanghai Bank, 1 Queen's Road Central, Hong Kong, 011-852/5-8682388.

$ COST-CUTTING TIP #81
For Swiss Banking, Try Nordfinanz, Overland Bank or Ueberseebank

One Swiss bank I have found to be most reasonable is Nordfinanz Bank. With a branch in the Bahamas, it's also convenient for Americans. Here are some of its charges:

- Foreign currencies (both in spot and forward markets): 0.3% commission on the market value of each transaction.
- Precious metals: Same as foreign currencies.
- Stocks and bonds: A brokerage fee of 0.3% plus third-party charges are debited to the client for each purchase and sale, plus normal brokerage expenses abroad, with a minimum charge of $60. To hold the securities in safe custody, on your behalf, an annual safekeeping fee of 0.4% is charged.

- Managed accounts: $350,000 minimum. An extra fee of 0.3% per year is charged.
- Minimums: $20,000 for private clients and $100,000 for corporations.

For more information and a brochure describing its fees in greater detail, write to: Nordfinanz Bank Zurich, Nassau Branch, Norfolk House, Frederick Street, P.O. Box N-7529, Nassau, Bahamas, 809/32-33347, fax: 809/32-82177.

Overland Bank

Another bank that's readily accessible to Americans is Overland Bank, which has a representative office in Vancouver, British Columbia. Its fees are comparable, in many areas, to those at Nordfinanz. Here are some of its charges:

- Certificates of deposit: Available in ten currencies, with durations of 3, 6, 9 and 12 months; no tax on interest earnings. Minimum: $20,000; commission: 0.125% per quarter.
- Fiduciary time deposits: From 2 to 365 days in duration; no tax on interest earnings. Minimum: $50,000; commission: 0.0625% per month.
- Eurobonds: No withholding tax on interest earnings. Minimum: $5,000; commission: 0.375%

The bank also offers several precious metals accounts:

- Custodial account: For long-term physical ownership of metals in segregated storage; client retains full ownership. Minimum initial purchase: $5,000; maximum commission: 1%; storage fee: 0.4% per year.
- Claim account: For the active metals trader. Minimum initial purchase: $10,000; administrative fee: 0.3% per year.

The Overland Bank also offers a full range of securities investments. Safekeeping, which includes collection of dividends and interest, is 0.15% a year. In addition, it offers two low-load funds, both denominated in Swiss francs.

The minimum account opening amount for Overland Bank is US$20,000. For information, call or write: Overland Bank, P.O. Box 48326, Vancouver, BC V7X IAI, Canada, 604/682-3626, fax: 604/682-6643.

This is also probably the only Swiss bank that has a toll-free information line for the United States: 800/663-8942.

Ueberseebank in Zurich

Another Swiss bank with excellent services and low charges is Ueberseebank. Whether small or large, the investor will find Ueberseebank an extremely useful bank. It has especially good relations with U.S. investors. Minimum investment to open a Swiss-franc savings account is only $3,000. It also offers multicurrency checking accounts, accounts in precious metals, stocks, bonds, mutual funds and managed accounts. Contact: Ueberseebank, Limmatquai 2, CH-8024 Zurich, Switzerland, telephone: 011-411/252-0304.

$ COST-CUTTING TIP #82
For More Information on Finding
and Using a Swiss Bank . . .

An excellent new book available on Swiss banks is *Swiss Bank Accounts: A Personal Guide to Ownership, Benefits, and Use* by Michael Arthur Jones, a U.S. accountant. Published in 1990, it's filled with useful information on choosing and getting the utmost from your Swiss bank. You can order from TAB Books, Inc., Blue Ridge Summit, PA 17294, 800/822-8158 or 717/794-2191. The cost is $22.95 (no postage and handling charge if prepaid).

$ COST-CUTTING TIP #83
The Best Low-Cost Way To Hold
Precious Metals in Switzerland

Although the charges for precious metals accounts at Overland Bank are quite reasonable, I don't recommend them for most people. A better way is through Mocatta Metals Delivery Orders.

Mocatta Metals certificates are negotiable warehouse receipts for gold (or silver) stored safely in your own name in Zurich, Switzerland. According to tax experts, the metals certificate is not considered a foreign bank account, so there is no need to report its existence to the government. Because you send funds to a domestic dealer, there's no requirement to report money sent overseas. And because the certificates are nonnegotiable, you can carry them in and out of the United States without having to declare them to customs.

Mocatta Metals Delivery Orders are available for gold bullion coins in units of 10 American Eagles, 10 Canadian Maple Leafs, 10 Mexican 50 Pesos or 10 Austrian (or Hungarian) Coronas. If you prefer gold bullion to coins, bars are available in 100 or 400 troy ounces. Silver units are available in 500 1-ounce silver Eagles, 400 1-ounce Canadian silver Maple Leafs, or 10 100-ounce bars.

Using these warehouse receipts, you can present your certificate in Zurich and take delivery of your gold or silver if you wish. It's only a taxable event if you sell your gold or silver, not if you take delivery. Your stored metals are insured by Lloyd's of London. There's a 0.05% per annum charge for storage and insurance. That's only slightly more than some Swiss banks charge for storing metals, but I believe the extra benefits are well worth the small added cost.

You can obtain the Mocatta Metals Delivery Orders from two reputable dealers:

- Benham Certified Metals, 1665 Charleston Rd., Mountain View, CA 94043, 800/447-4653 or 415/965-4275.
- Rhyne Precious Metals, 425 Pike St., Suite 403, Seattle, WA 98101, 800/426-7835 or 206/623-6900.

$ COST-CUTTING TIP #84
For Small Investors, Austria May Be Best

Austrian banks may be better for the small investor.

One Austrian bank geared to the smaller U.S. investor is Royal Trust Bank, P.O. Box 306, A-1011 Vienna, Austria, 011-43-1/43 61 61. Here's a rundown on some of its fees:

- Foreign currencies: Interest-bearing accounts are available in several currencies. Accounts can be totally or partially switched from one currency to another at a 0.25% currency conversion fee (minimum fee: US$5). However, any time you make a deposit to a checking or savings account, currency conversion (if desired) is free of charge.
- Precious metals: Sold at the Zurich or London market price, plus a commission of 1% on silver and 0.5% on other precious metals, with a minimum commission of $20 or equivalent. Annual storage and insurance charges are 0.35% on silver and 0.25% on market value of holdings. On bullion coins, like the Canadian Maple Leaf or American Eagle, there is no commission; you pay the spread between bid and ask. The annual storage charge is 0.35%.
- Precious metals forward and futures contracts: Expect the same commission charged on forward contracts as on the spot purchases. Futures contracts are also available, with a $3,000 minimum margin requirement per contract and a commission of US$150 per round turn. There are also checking accounts in precious metals.
- Stocks and bonds: A safe custody account is available for stocks and bonds. Any securities you transfer to or purchase through the safe custody account segregate from the bank's assets and remain your direct property. Commissions are 0.75% on bonds, for purchases of up to $50,000, and 0.6% for purchases over that amount ($30 minimum). For stocks and mutual funds, commissions are 1.25% on purchases up $50,000 and 1.0% on purchases above that. If transactions are executed outside Austria, applicable foreign

brokerage charges will be added. The annual safe custody fee for securities is 0.25% ($10 minimum); larger safe custody accounts are subject to special rates.

- Managed accounts: The fee is 1% of market value, charged on a prorated basis at the end of each month. Minimums are only US$10,000.

$ COST-CUTTING TIP #85
For Larger Investors, Try Luxembourg or the Channel Islands

Luxembourg and the Channel Islands may be even better than Austria or Switzerland for larger investors. Here are some contacts:

- Kredietbank, boulevarde Roual 43, L-2955, Luxembourg, 011-352/47971.
- Bank of Butterfield International (Guernsey) Limited, P.O. Box 25, Hadsley House, Lefebvre St., St. Peters Port, Guernsey, Channel Islands, U.K., 011-44/481-711521, fax: 011-44/481-7144533. This is a wholly owned subsidiary of the Bank of N. T. Butterfield & Son Ltd., in Bermuda.
- Lloyd's Bank in London. Its high-interest checking account is one of the most-flexible banking vehicles I have ever seen. Not only do you get a high yield, but as a nonresident, you are exempt from British withholding tax. You receive a checkbook and a VISA debit card for instant access to your money in the United States and around the world. You can earn even more if you choose not to have checking privileges. Minimum investment: $2,000. For information contact: Lloyd's Bank, 39 Threadneedle St., London EC2R 8AU, England, 011-44-71/628-7755.

$ COST-CUTTING TIP #86
Buy Low-Cost and No-Load
Offshore Mutual Funds

The largest mutual fund manager in the world is also one of the least expensive. Based in Holland, the Robeco Group operates as a cooperative; the company is owned by its investors. Management fees run around 0.3% annually.

The firm has a plan called the Geneva Account, which starts at minimums of US$5,000. For more information, write or call: Robeco Geneva Plan, Case Postale 114, CH 1215 Geneva 15-Aeroport, Switzerland, 011-41/22-41-1297.

Another no-load fund is the Assetmix Umbrella Fund, managed by Commercial Union Assurance Co., one of the largest insurance companies in England. It has 14 subfunds, and you can allocate your investment among them. The fund is domiciled in Luxembourg, which has no income or capital gains tax other than a Luxembourg tax of 0.06% annually.

There is no initial sales charge, but there is a fee payable to the professional advisors, which is deducted from the money received. This is normally 0.5%. The annual charges are 1.4% on equity funds and 1.275% on the bond and reserve (currency) funds. There is also no bid-ask spread; each fund's price is based on net asset value. You can switch instantly among the subfunds by phone, fax or mail.

You can buy Assetmix through the Royal Trust Bank, P.O. Box 306, A-1011, Vienna, Austria, 011-43-1/43 61 61. The problem is that if you buy through Assetmix, you will pay a commission of 1.25% (or 1% for investments of over US$50,000). An alternative is to buy direct. The problem here is that the fund will not sell to those with a U.S. address, since it is not registered with the SEC. In order to buy the fund, you will need to establish an address outside the United States. You could, for example, receive information through a friend or relative living abroad. You could also receive it through a bank, but the bank might want to charge a fee.

If you're interested, you can reach the fund at Assetmix, 7th Fl.,

Centre Mercure, 41 avenue de la Gare, L-1611 Luxembourg, Grand Duchy of Luxembourg, 011-352/48 90 61, fax: 011-352/ 49 23 69.

Another no-load umbrella fund is the Gartmore Fund. You can get information from Gartmore Fund Managers, c/o Gartmore Luxembourg, 23 rue des Bruyeres, L-1274 Luxembourg, 011-352/ 465-4241.

$ COST-CUTTING TIP #87
Subscribe to the *Financial Times* and Specialized Newsletters

The best way to keep abreast of foreign investments is through the *Financial Times*, a daily newspaper that lists most offshore funds. It's available in most large libraries, or contact: *Financial Times*, 14 E. 60th St., P.H., New York, NY 10022, in the United States, 800/ 628-8088 or in Canada, 800/543-1007.

In addition, Gary Scott publishes two excellent newsletters on foreign investments. *Fund Help International* ($149 per year) covers the international mutual funds, while *Gary Scott's World Reports* ($99 per year) talks about the full range of investment opportunities overseas. If you mention this book, you can get a free sample copy on request or the three most-current issues for $10. Contact: International Service Center, 3106 Tamiami Trail North, Naples, FL 33940.

One other U.S. newsletter that covers the foreign markets well is *Dessauer's Journal of Finanical Markets*, P.O. Box 1718, Orleans, MA 02653, 800/272-7550, $195 per year, 24 issues, plus hotline.

Of course, I also bring you the best ideas in overseas investing each month in *Forecasts & Strategies*, 7811 Montrose Rd., Potomac, MD 20854, 800/777-5005, $99 special introductory offer for the first year (regularly $179 per year).

CHAPTER 13

Lowest-Cost Methods of Borrowing Money To Invest

Want to make a million dollars? Borrow a million and pay it off!

—Jack Miller

It's NOT always wise to borrow too much money to invest. Over-leveraging is what got Donald Trump into trouble. Anybody can become a *millionaire*, on paper, if they borrow enough money. Still, there may be times when you'll want to leverage your investments. Just be prudent. True Scrooges build *real* wealth—not just paper profits.

$ COST-CUTTING TIP #88
Your Discount Broker: Best Source for Low-Cost Funds

Want to borrow below the prime rate? Try your stockbroker. Stockbrokers will loan money at the *broker's call rate*. It's usually about 0.5% to 1% below the prime rate, which is the rate at which banks are said to lend to their best customers.

All you need to do to borrow at the broker's call rate is to have marginable securities in a margin account. All the discount brokers listed in chapter 3 offer margin accounts. Simply fill out their form, and you can borrow money against the securities in your account. But don't overdo it.

$ COST-CUTTING TIP #89
Seven Ways To Raise a Down Payment on Real Estate

If you can't seem to accumulate enough capital to raise a down payment, here are some creative possibilities you may not be aware of:

1. Lease with an option to buy—just make sure you get a rent credit toward the down payment.
2. If you or your spouse is eligible, get a VA mortgage that requires no down payment.
3. Get a VA mortgage that requires only a low down payment.
4. Buy a foreclosed VA or FHA home that requires no, or only a low, down payment.
5. When dealing with an investor, get a second mortgage note for all or part of the down payment money you need. Negotiate a favorable interest rate.
6. Offer some unnecessary item—like a second car, boat or RV—as a down payment.
7. Try a shared-equity down payment. Some real estate brokers and mortgage companies are linking well-heeled investors with cash-strapped home buyers. Both parties benefit. The buyer has someone to share the down payment; the investor shares in any rise in home values and may collect additional fees.

$ COST-CUTTING TIP #90
Consider a Home Equity Loan

Interest rates on home equity loans are higher than the prime rate, and initial charges are high. But rates are lower than credit cards, and you can also deduct the interest. Shop around for the best rate, starting at your credit union (if you belong to one), where loans are generally cheaper (although maturities may be shorter and the credit line smaller).

$ COST-CUTTING TIP #91
Borrow from Your Company's Retirement Plan

Again, interest rates here are better than credit cards—generally, one percentage point above the prime rate. What's more, credit checks are rare, and the interest you pay will, in a sense, go back into your own pocket.

Unfortunately, consumer interest, for the most part, is not deductible from your income tax; the amount you can borrow is limited to $50,000; and payments can be high, because the loans are short term. Furthermore, you must repay the loan if you leave your job. If you don't, the outstanding balance becomes taxable income. Check with your company to get details.

$ COST-CUTTING TIP #92
As a Last Resort—Tap Your Credit Cards

Using your credit card to get investment money is one-step away from going to a pawnbroker or a loan shark. Interest rates are usually above 18%. Don't do it unless it's absolutely necessary, and if you do, make sure you use the lowest-interest credit card you can find. You can get up-to-date lists of credit cards with no annual fees ($1.50), and with the lowest interest rates ($1.50), by sending a check ($3.00 for both lists) to Bankcardholders of America, 560 Herndon Parkway, Suite 120, Herndon, VA 22070, 800/638-6407.

$ COST-CUTTING TIP #93
Low-Interest Loans from
the Largest Retail Outlet

Sears's Discover card offers potentially low-interest loans on its cash advances and cash advance checks. Until recently, it offered a 25-day grace period on its cash advances, with a maximum one-time charge of $10 but quickly eliminated this source of interest-free money in early 1992. Sears replaced the grace period with a fee schedule for each new cash advance as follows:

$500.00 or less	2.5%
$500.01–$1,000.00	2.0%
Over $1,000.00	1.5%

Now this may sound like no bargain if you borrowed monthly from your Discover card—the interest charges could vary between 18% and 30%!

Here's how you can reduce those interest charges to 9% per annum: First, always borrow more than $1,000. That way you'll be charged only 1.5% on the cash advance. Second, take out a cash advance the day after your Discover card closing date. This will give you a maximum of 55 days' (almost two months) use of the money before you have to pay it back. Using this method, you could borrow several thousand dollars during the year and pay the 1.5% cash advance fee only six times, reducing your total cost to 9.0% annually. This is a bargain compared to the normal interest cost of personal unsecured loans from banks (usually 14% to 18%).

Discover's cash advance checks are extremely flexible. You can use them to make purchases or investments of any kind, including stocks, gold, real estate or foreign investments.

As for the 1.5% transaction fee for cash advances, you can offset that amount by simply using the Discover card to make purchases. Every time you buy something with the Discover card, you earn up to 1% in cash, which is paid in a check to you at the end of each year! (Anything over $3,000 per year earns a 1% rebate, with less than 1% for the first $3,000.)

Suppose you charged $1,000 on average each month during the year. At the end of the year, you would get a check for nearly $120 from Discover—enough to offset the transaction fees on your cash advance loan. Thus, both Sears and you benefit—you with low-interest loans, and Sears with increased volume on its Discover card. The only deterrent to earning a large cash bonus is that Discover is not universally accepted. It is accepted at Sears and a growing number of other chains, but it is not yet readily as accepted as VISA or MasterCard.

Discover card applications are available at local Sears stores or by calling: 1/800/DISCOVER.

$ COST-CUTTING TIP #94
Low-Interest Loans from the Largest Telephone Company

AT&T has matched Sears's low-interest loans by offering cash advance convenience checks through its Universal card. The Universal card is linked through the MasterCard network, so the card can be used practically anywhere.

Currently the Universal card offers a 25-day grace period on all cash advances, as long as your current balance is paid in full. The only charge is a 2.5% transaction fee when you use a cash advance or convenience check, but the charge is limited to a *maximum* $20 per transaction! In order to keep your costs of borrowing down, it pays to borrow substantial sums.

You have 25 to 55 days before you have to pay off the cash advance. After that, you are charged daily interest.

To obtain an AT&T Universal card, call: 800/423-4343 or the local AT&T operator.

▶*Note:* Like the Sears Discover card, AT&T may change its cash advance policy at any time. Please check before acting on this advice.

Incidentally, the Universal card has many other benefits besides low-interest cash advances—10% discount on long distance calls, superdiscounts on international calls made to the United States when you are traveling abroad, free flight insurance, etc.

Another credit card company that offers a 25-day grace period on cash advances—with no finance charges if you pay off by the due date, and if there is no outstanding balance on your account—is Fidelity National Bank (800/753-2900). It offers either VISA or MasterCard, with a 17.9% interest rate on the unpaid balance. The only other charge is a fee of 4% on the loan (cash advance), up to a maximum charge of $25. That means the effective monthly interest on a $5,000 cash advance is only 0.5% (6% per year) if you pay it off by the due date. But check with Fidelity National Bank on its current policy—it could change at any time.

CHAPTER 14

Cutting Your Biggest Investment Costs—Taxes!

There will never be a tax law without legal loopholes!

—LARRY ABRAHAM

EVERY COST-CONSCIOUS Scrooge investor faces four major enemies: (1) bad investment advice, (2) high fees and commissions, (3) inflation and (4) taxes. Investors worldwide recognize early on that taxes can easily be the highest portfolio expense. Each year inflation may cut the value of your portfolio by 10%, but taxes can take a much bigger bite—as much as 35% or more, depending on where you live.

Uncle Sam used to give a variety of tax breaks for investors. Prior to 1986, long-term capital gains were taxed at only 20%, there was a $200 dividend exclusion, most people qualified for IRAs, etc. All that's gone. Today, there are few exemptions on capital gains, interest or dividends. The marginal tax rate on capital gains is 28% and higher for interest and dividend income, and that's not counting the additional taxes by state and local governments. Uncle Sam discourages Uncle Scrooge's investment plans so much that he is likely to find better opportunities in Asia, Europe and other foreign places, where the investment atmosphere is more conducive to making money. (Germany, by the way, still has a long-term capital gains tax rate of *zero*!)

One of the worst problems facing investors is the taxation of phantom income. This irksome situation occurs frequently with holders of certificates of deposit, zero- coupon bonds and mutual funds (via annual distributions). Let's face it—Uncle Sam is no friend of investors.

Four Ways To Beat Uncle Sam

But wait! Loopholes abound in even the most complex and onerous tax system. Fortunately, the IRS permits several methods of beating the taxman. You must use these tax-free vehicles if you are going to protect your assets from the IRS. Here are four legal ways for Scrooge investors to buy and sell tax free:

$ COST-CUTTING TIP #95
Set Up a Self-Directed,
IRS-Approved Pension Program

Self-directed programs include IRAs, self-employed retirement accounts and corporate pension plans. Company-directed plans limit your choice of investments, but self-directed plans through brokerage accounts allow maximum freedom, including foreign investments. All income and profits are tax deferred until you withdraw them for retirement.

Chapter 3 lists the seven best nationwide brokerage firms. Most of them charge an annual fee for an IRA or other self-directed retirement plans. For example, Fidelity Brokerage Services charges $30 per year; Charles Schwab & Co., $22 per year; and Jack White & Co., $35 per year. But don't be penny-wise and pound-foolish. Select the discounter that offers you the best deal for all the services you will need, especially commissions on trades. Since you can switch between investments all you want without tax consequences, you may be doing a lot of trading. The commissions you generate will undoubtedly exceed manyfold the annual cost of an IRA or other pension plan.

$ COST-CUTTING TIP #96
Invest in a Low-Cost Variable Annuity

Variable annuities offer another way to invest in a variety of investments without paying current taxes. There are many from which to choose.

At this writing, Vanguard's Variable Annuity offers the lowest cost of any annuity available. Its expense ratio is approximately 1% per annum, including insurance administration, compared to 2% to 3% for most other variable annuities. It also has no up-front load or early withdrawal penalties.

Currently, the investment choices are limited to four funds—a managed stock fund, a stock index fund, a high-grade bond fund and a money market fund. You can switch from one fund to another at any time without penalty or tax consequences. Minimum investment: $5,000. Contact: Vanguard, P.O. Box 2600, Valley Forge, PA 19482, 800/522-5555.

You might also want to check out Scudder's Horizon Plan, a variable annuity with seven fund options, including its top-performing international fund. Annual expense ratio is 1.5%, slightly higher than Vanguard's. Scudder offers unlimited telephone switching. Minimum investment: $2,500. Contact: Scudder, 160 Federal St., Boston, MA 02110, 800/225-2470.

$ COST-CUTTING TIP #97
Sell Your Investment, Pay No Capital Gains Tax and Get a Tax Deduction to Boot!

Here's a great way to avoid the capital gains tax completely, get a tax deduction and secure more spendable income at the same time.

This technique is especially beneficial to retirees or people about to retire. You may have growth stocks and real estate that you want to sell. They may not pay much in income and now that you are retired you need more income.

Suppose you own growth stocks that you bought 15 years ago for $20,000, with a current market value of $150,000. Like most growth stocks, they pay only a small dividend, say 2%, so your growth stocks are currently paying you a low $3,000 a year. But now you want more income. You would like to sell your growth stocks and buy high-yielding bonds, which at 10% would pay you $15,000 a year. But there's a problem. If you switch from stocks to bonds, you'll pay 28% of the capital gains to Uncle Sam (plus more to the state you live in).

Since your cost basis is $20,000, you have a long-term capital gain of $130,000. You'll owe the IRS a whopping $36,400—thousands of dollars lost forever. If you invested the remaining funds in an account paying 10%, you would earn $11,360 a year—substantially more than $3,000, but much less than the $15,000 you would get annually if you didn't have to pay the capital gains tax at all.

Here's the ideal solution: Establish a special tax-exempt trust called a charitable remainder trust (CRT). Using a CRT, you donate your property to your favorite alma mater, church or charity, and obtain a lifetime income from it. But a new type of CRT is now available that is far more flexible than the old ones. I'm referring to a new CRT where you can be your own trustee, make contributions at any time and even change your beneficiaries during your lifetime.

Using the above example, let's see how valuable this new CRT can be. You transfer the growth stocks to your CRT, and the trustee (you) sells them through a broker. By using this trust vehicle, the CRT completely avoids the capital gains tax. In addition, you receive an immediate tax deduction for setting up this charitable trust. The deduction is determined by IRS tables and depends on your age and amount of investment.

As trustee of the CRT, you can then purchase an income fund and pay yourself 10% a year in income—in this case, a full $15,000 each year for the rest of your life.

If you have additional stocks, real estate or other assets you wish to sell, you can donate them to the same trust and boost your lifetime income further.

When you die, the assets in the CRT go to your favorite charity, whether it be your alma mater, a church, a hospital or a public foundation. In this special CRT, you can name one or several charitable organizations as beneficiaries. As an added bonus, these assets going to charity are not subject to federal estate taxes.

You can start your own CRT with as little as $2,000, and add to it as often as you like. Each time you do, you'll get an annual tax deduction, avoid capital gains taxes and obtain more spendable income. The cost is a one-time setup fee of $300, plus an annual administrative fee based on the market value of the trust's assets (ranging from 0.8% to as little as $0.12 per $1,000).

Contact David T. Phillips & Co., Independent Insurance Specialist, 3200 N. Dobson Rd., Building C, Chandler, AZ 85224, 800/223-9610 or 602/897-6088, fax: 602/897-9599.

$ COST-CUTTING TIP #98
Invest in a Foreign Roll-Up Mutual Fund

In chapter 12 on foreign investments, I wrote about foreign *roll-up mutual funds*. A good example is Assetmix, an umbrella group of roll-up funds trading on the Luxembourg Stock Exchange, managed by Commercial Union, one of the largest British insurance companies. There are 14 subfunds in Assetmix, offering stock investments in the United States, Europe and Asia, global bond investments and gold stocks. They are called roll-up funds because none of them declares any dividends or capital gains. Distributions are simply added to each fund's net asset value. Thus, you pay no taxes until you sell the funds. Switching between subfunds is permitted.

▶*Note:* To discourage Americans from investing in foreign roll-up funds, Congress recently imposed a penalty on taxpayers who invest in them. When you sell the foreign fund, profits are subject to an interest penalty, in addition to the normal capital gains tax. However, the tax and surcharge are not due until you sell the fund. Hence, offshore funds remain an excellent tax-deferral vehicle. You can hold the roll-up fund for 10, 20 or more years and avoid taxes entirely.

$ COST-CUTTING TIP #99
Use Tax Strategies Outside Tax-Free Vehicles

The following strategies can minimize your taxes outside a pension or other tax-free vehicle:

- Sell stocks, bonds and other investments that have declined in value since you bought them. Losers can be used to offset gains you have made during the year.
- Give appreciated property to your children over age 13. You can transfer income to them by giving them appreciated assets. When they sell the assets, they report the gain and pay the taxes at *their* lower tax rate.
- Use a tax-free exchange of real estate or insurance policy or real estate property; check with your tax advisor about a *like-kind exchange*.

In fact, there are so many little-known techniques to avoid investment taxes that Vern Jacobs, former editor of *Tax Angles* and a CPA, has put together the definitive guide for tax-wise investors. The second edition of *The Zero Tax Portfolio Manual* has just been published. This 212-page oversized how-to manual lists hundreds of practical ways to reduce and eliminate taxes on interest, dividends and capital gains. The book discusses how to avoid the capital gains tax, charitable giving, year-end tax strategies and tax deductions for investors. Get your copy by sending $49.50 to Research Press, Inc., P.O. Box 8137, Prairie Village, KS 66208, 800/800-3510 or 913/383-3535, fax: 913/383-3505.

$ COST-CUTTING TIP #100
How To Find the Lowest-Cost Tax Preparer

The cheapest way to do your taxes is to do them yourself. Several excellent low-cost tax manuals are available to help you. The best ones are the annuals put together by J. K. Lasser & Co., H&R Block and the Arthur Young accounting firm, available in most major bookstores in January.

These are sufficient for most people, particularly if your income is mostly salary and your deductions are easy to compute.

The next most expensive resource is the store-front tax-preparer, such as the H&R Block chain. Preparation fees should be well under $100. But don't expect any tax-planning advice. Most of the people working in these offices are part-timers, hired at tax time. H&R Block and similar firms also offer full-time preparers but expect to pay at least $100 for their services.

The third option is an enrolled agent. Enrolled agents must either have five years of continuous employment with the IRS, applying and interpreting the tax code, or else they must pass a two-day exam on taxes for individuals, small businesses, partnerships and corporations. They also must take 30 hours of continuous education every year.

If you're self-employed, you may benefit from having an enrolled agent. It's best, of course, to get referrals from friends and relatives. You can also get a referral in your area from the National Association of Enrolled Agents (800/424-4339 or 301/984-6232). But stay away from any enrolled agent, or for that matter any other tax preparer, who guarantees a refund or whose fee is a percentage of the refund.

Fourth are certified public accountants (CPAs). They'll probably cost 25% more than enrolled agents, but they're often worth it. CPAs are usually best for those people who want to be more aggressive in their tax planning. Enrolled agents generally are more conservative. Again, personal referrals are the best way to find them.

Highest priced are tax attorneys. Their fees can run in the hundreds of dollars per hour. Generally, I don't recommend tax attorneys to prepare returns. Use your CPA or enrolled agent for that. (Attorneys lose their client privilege if they do your tax return.) You should use your tax attorney to represent you, if necessary, before the IRS, especially if your return is complicated or involves large sums of money, even though he or she did not file your return. I've found that tax attorneys are worth their weight in gold in tax disputes with the IRS. They are far more intimidating than CPAs!

$ COST-CUTTING TIP #101
Low-Cost Tax-Cutting Ploy for
Precious Metals and Rare Coins

Did you buy precious metals or rare coins years ago at high prices? Would you like to hang onto them and still take a tax deduction for your losses? Here's what you can do.

Precious metals and rare coins do not fall under the wash-sales rule for securities. That means that you can sell your metals or coins, buy them back immediately and still have a legitimate tax loss locked in for the rest of the year. Ordinarily, commissions for this type of trade would be prohibitive. But there's one dealer who will do it for a nominal fee.

Guardian International will handle the transaction for 2% (for metals) or 4% (for rare coins), plus shipping. Normally, you would pay at least double that amount. For information, contact: Guardian International, Inc., 2499 N. Harrison St., Arlington, VA 22207, 800/642-2208 or 703/237-1133.

Happy tax-free investing!

CHAPTER 15

Other Ways To Slash Your Investment Costs: Investment Clubs, Financial Planners and Partnerships

Human felicity is produced not so much by great pieces of good fortune that seldom happen as by little advantages that occur every day.

—BEN FRANKLIN

THE LIST of ways you can cut investment costs is limited only by the imagination. The wise miser can find countless techniques. Here are a few more. Be resourceful.

$ COST-CUTTING TIP #102
Join a Club for Discounts

A few organizations offer you dozens of ways to reduce your investment costs. Here are some clubs that offer substantial benefits to investors:

- American Association of Individual Investors (AAII), 625 North Michigan Ave., Chicago, IL 60611, 312/280-0170. This nonprofit organization offers several benefits to members, including a free monthly journal, a quote line that gives real-time price quotes on stocks, options and mutual funds, some 46 local chapters, several free books, reduced-cost investment seminars and discounts on other services, like its study programs and computer users newsletter. Dues are only $49 per year, and if you are not happy with your membership, you can withdraw at any time and get a complete refund. If you like it, you can sign up for a lifetime membership for $450.
- American Association of Retired Persons (AARP), 601 E St., NW, Washington, D.C. 20049, 202/434-2277. It's not really an investment club, but because of its nonprofit status, the AARP can offer a variety of cut-rate services. To investors, it offers seven no-load funds managed by the big mutual fund firm Scudder, which has IRAs and Keogh plans with no custodial fees. A large-print prospectus is available.

  AARP also offers a VISA card from Bank One, with a low annual fee of $10 and a low 15.6% annual percentage rate, plus a long-term commitment to keep that rate low. Health, auto, homeowner and medical insurance is also available. Membership is only $5 per year and is open to anyone 50 or over.
- National Association of Investors Clubs (NAIC), 1515 East Eleven Mile Rd., Royal Oak, MI 48067, 313/543-0612. Since 1951, this organization has helped small investors to form clubs to study the stock market and invest in common stocks. It offers a wide variety of publications and services at modest prices. It also offers discounts on group insurance plans and study-travel trips. Write for a brochure.
- USAA, USAA Building, San Antonio, TX 78288, 800/531-8080 or 512/498-8080. Founded in 1922, this is a huge member-owned cooperative offering low costs on insurance and other financial services. *Forbes* magazine once described it as "a financial supermarket—a one-stop shop for everything from stocks to life insurance."

Membership is open to active or former military officers and their dependents, but you don't have to be a member to take advantage of most of the investment services. Some life and health insurance, pure no-load mutual funds, banking services, real estate products and the discount brokerage service are all available to nonmembers. However, only members and associate members are eligible for the casualty and property insurance products and for the buying club.

$ COST-CUTTING TIP #103
Use Fee-Only Financial Planners

If you need expert help in putting together a financial plan, it's best to go to a fee-only planner. You're likely to pay far less, in the long run, for a planner who charges a flat or hourly fee than you will for one who makes a living by selling high-commission products. As always, it's a good idea to shop around—talk to at least three financial planners.

Fee-only planners are sometimes hard to find. Expect to pay from $100 to $175 an hour and a minimum of $2,500 total for a comprehensive plan. You should always get references, and check them out before putting down any money. Of course, you can get lower-cost plans, including some computerized plans. But, these usually leave you to do most of the work.

You can find a fee-only planner through the National Association of Personal Financial Advisors, 8140 Knue Rd., Suite 110, Indianapolis, IN 46250, 800/366-2732 or 708/537-7722. Call or write to them for a referral in your area. Also ask for your free copy of a list of tough questions to ask prospective planners.

There's just one problem with a fee-only planner. Some of them go beyond recommending investments and actually structure investment deals. They may not be earning a commission, but they still stand to gain by charging management and other fees. If any planner recommends a limited partnership, make sure he or she doesn't have an interest in it.

$ COST-CUTTING TIP #104
Don't Pay More than a 10% to 12% Load
for a New Limited Partnership

Some of the worst abuses in the securities industry occur in partnerships. Loads average 20% and can exceed 40% in some tax credit deals. The state of Washington is not approving partnerships where total loads exceed 10%. (If it's not registered in Washington State, don't get involved.)

Not surprisingly, the worst deals are usually the ones with the highest costs. The better underwriters steer clear of those general partners with bad track records, forcing them to seek out the more aggressive underwriters, who charge more to raise funds.

One of my recommended brokers, Rick Rule of Torrey Pines Securities (800/356-8973 or 619/259-9921), refuses to sell partnerships with loads exceeding 12.5%. He might be a good place to start if you're in the market for a partnership.

$ COST-CUTTING TIP #105
Partnership Investors: Do Your Homework

I don't generally recommend private-placement limited partnerships for most people. You have not only to meet strict financial suitability standards but also to be a sophisticated investor. You need to be able to read and understand long, complicated and jargon-filled prospectuses. Pay especially close attention to *up-front costs* (organization and sales costs), management fees and overhead and the track record of the general partner.

$ COST-CUTTING TIP #106
Shop the Secondary Market for
Big Discounts on Partnerships

The secondary market for partnerships is a buyer's market. People who bought partnerships in the 1980s, when they were popular, have seen their investment get clobbered by changes in tax law and the investment markets. Some will sell at almost any price. Other partnerships sold in the secondary market are distressed sales, as a result of death, divorce, bankruptcy and so forth.

It's possible to buy a partnership for less than 50% of the value of the underlying assets, though discounts of around 30% are far more common. However, there aren't any newsletters or publications that cover this market—it's too small. You have to ferret out the deals on your own. You've got to be a knowledgeable investor and a shrewd negotiator in this market.

A good place to start is with those firms that are active in the secondary market. Each firm operates differently. Some only work with private individuals through brokers. Others merely match buyers and sellers, charging a processing fee. Still others make their money by buying for their own inventory and marking up the price to buyers—sometimes as much as 20%. Here are some of the major players:

- Chicago Partnership Board, Inc., 800/272-6273 or 312/332-4100
- Dunhill Equities, 800/937-0550 or 516/747-5904
- Frain Asset Management, 800/654-6110 or 813/397-2701
- MacKenzie Securities, 800/854-8357
- National Partnership Exchange, 800/356-2739, in Florida, 800/ 336-2739
- Nationwide Partnership Marketplace, 800/969-8996
- Partnership Secur. Exchange, Inc., 800/736-9797 or 813/397-2701
- Raymond James & Associates, Inc., 800/248-8863
- G.K. Scott & Co., 800/526-1763

CHAPTER 16

The Cheapskate's Guide to Unlimited, Free Investment Information

You have before you wealth untold . . . the best things in life are free.

GOOD NEWS

INVESTMENT INFORMATION doesn't come cheap. One newsletter on annual reports sells for $12,000 a year. Most of the better investment newsletters are priced at over $100 per year. Often, this is money well spent. But, as Uncle Scrooge himself might say, if you can get the information either free or at a cut rate, why pay the full price?

$ COST-CUTTING TIP: #107
Tap into an Almost Unlimited Source of Free Investment Information

One place where you can get almost unlimited information on investments is your local public library and, in college towns, the college library (often open to the public).

Virtually all libraries—even the small ones—get the *Wall Street Journal* and the major business magazines: *Forbes, Business Week, Barron's, U.S. News & World Report, Money, Changing Times* and *The Economist.* My favorite is *Forbes*; it's the most irreverent and hardest hitting of the group.

Less well known is the fact that many libraries also have subscriptions to the larger investment advisory services, like *Value Line* and *Standard & Poor's.* These are invaluable sources of unbiased information on hundreds of stocks.

An excellent source of information on mutual funds, available in many libraries, is the *Weisenberger Mutual Funds Investment Report* and its companion publications.

In some major metropolitan areas, the libraries subscribe to a selection of financial newsletters, by the top Wall Street and hard-money gurus—from Larry Abraham to Martin Zweig!

Then, there are investment books. With the price of most hardback books over $20, you can save a lot of money here. With interlibrary loan, you can use your local library to borrow books from almost any library in the country. Ask your librarian for details. Interlibrary loan is especially useful if you're researching, say, an obscure collectible and need to find everything ever written on it. It's also a real money saver, as books on art, antiques and collectibles can cost over $50.

Last, don't ignore your librarian—not only a money saver but a time saver. Your librarian knows her or his way around the library and can usually put a finger on a piece of information faster than you can. What's more, most libraries will answer simple questions over the phone—if it's something like looking up an address or a telephone number. And they're always pleased to help. After all, that's what you're paying your taxes for.

$ COST-CUTTING TIP #108
Cut-Rate Newsletter Subscriptions

One firm will arrange cut-rate trial subscriptions to leading financial newsletters. This is an inexpensive way to sample dozens of newsletters, and to see which ones you like, at savings far lower than what you would pay for a trial subscription to even one newsletter.

For a free catalog describing the trial-issue packages available, write to: Select Information Exchange, 244 W. 54th St., Room 714, New York, NY 10019, 212/247-7123.

$ COST-CUTTING TIP #109
Twenty-Four More Newsletters
You Can Get for Free!

Most newsletter publishers will send a free sample if you write or call asking for one. Some of them don't like to publicize it—they're afraid they might get deluged with requests. In preparing this book, we've located several that said they would be happy to offer free sample copies to readers of our book. Some of these are offered by special arrangement only, so make sure you mention this book when requesting.

- *Bob Nurock's Advisory*, P.O. Box 988, Paoli, PA 19301, 800/227-8883 or 215/296-2411. $247 per year, 17 issues, plus hotline. Edited by Robert Nurock, formerly a regular panelist on Louis Rukeyser's weekly television show "Wall Street Week." The newsletter provides analysis of the stock, bond and precious metals markets.
- *Czeschin's Mutual Fund Outlook*, P.O. Box 1423, Baltimore, MD 21203. $77 per year, 12 issues. Coverage of U.S. mutual funds.
- *Donoghue's Moneyletter*, 290 Eliot St., Ashland, MA 01742, 800/445-5900, in Massachusetts, 508/429-5930. $99 per year, 24 issues. Edited and published by best-selling financial author William Donoghue, this newsletter offers excellent coverage of no-load mutual funds.
- *Fabian's Telephone Switch*, P.O. Box 2538, Huntington Beach, CA 92647, 800/950-8765. $137 per year, 12 issues or $87 for a seven-month trial. Investment advisor Dick Fabian's simple system for trading no-load mutual funds.
- *The Financial Privacy Report*, Box 549, Bethel, CT 06801. $132

per year, 12 issues. Detailed how-to advice on all the legal ways to protect, preserve and enhance your financial privacy—and make low-profile profits as well.

- *Gary North's Remnant Review*, P.O. Box 84906, Phoenix, AZ 85071, 800/528-0559. $95, 22 issues. Economist North's unique perspective on the economy and the investment markets.
- *The G.E.O. Report*, P.O. Box 84906, Phoenix, AZ 85071, 800/528-0559. $199 per year, 24 issues. Larry Abraham's analysis of ecological and energy opportunities.
- *Gold Stocks Advisory*, P.O. Box 531, Bethel, CT 06801, 203/790-1694. $132 per year, 12 issues. Advice on mining stocks, by long-time precious metals expert Paul Sarnoff.
- *The Holt Advisory*, 2200 N. Florida Mango Rd., West Palm Beach, FL 33409, 800/289-9222 or 407/684-8100. $160 per year, 24 issues. Edited by long-time investment advisor Thomas J. Holt, contains specific strategies for stocks, utilities, precious metals and other markets.
- *Income & Safety*, 3741 North Federal Hwy., Ft. Lauderdale, FL 33306, 800/327-6720. $49 per year, 12 issues. Contains up-to-date information on the safest places to get the highest yield.
- *The Insiders*, 3741 North Federal Hwy., Ft. Lauderdale, FL 33306, 800/327-6720. $49 per year, 24 issues, plus hotline. Latest information and analysis on purchases and sales by corporate insiders.
- *Investor's Digest*, 3741 North Federal Hwy., Ft. Lauderdale, FL 33306, 800/327-6720. $29 per year, 12 issues, plus hotline that's updated daily. A monthly digest of what the major, top financial newsletters are saying.
- *Jay Schabacker's Mutual Fund Investing*, 7811 Montrose Rd., Potomac, MD 20854, 800/777-5005. $149 per year, 12 issues. Provides excellent advice on no-load mutual funds.
- *John Pugsley's Journal*, P.O. Box 471, Corona del Mar, CA 92625. Published irregularly, 8 to 12 times a year. $125, 12 issues. Economist Pugsley's thoughtful and insightful analysis of the economy and investment markets.
- *Larry Abraham's Insider Report*, P.O. Box 84906, Phoenix, AZ

85071, 800/528-0559. $199 per year, 12 issues. Abraham's unique blend of political analysis and investment advice.

- *Market Logic*, 3741 North Federal Hwy., Ft. Lauderdale, FL 33306, 800/327-6720. $95 per year, 24 issues, plus hotline. Editor Norman G. Fosback's recommendations and analysis of the investment markets.
- *Market Trim Tabs Triad*, P.O. Box 2949, Santa Rosa, CA 95405, 707/579-1712. Edited by Charles Biderman, this is one of the few newsletters on the market that offers advice on selling short.
- *Money & Markets: The Letter for Safety and Yield*, 2200 N. Florida Mango Rd., West Palm Beach, FL 33409, 800/289-9222. $160 per year, 12 issues. Editor Martin D. Weiss's newsletter on the economy and the investment markets.
- *Mutual Fund Forecaster*, 3741 North Federal Hwy., Ft. Lauderdale, FL 33306, 800/327-6720. $49 per year, 12 issues. Norman G. Fosback's advice on mutual funds, with an emphasis on the no-load and low-load funds.
- *New Issues*, 3741 North Federal Hwy., Ft. Lauderdale, FL 33306, 800/327-6720. $95 per year, 12 issues. An excellent way to keep abreast of what's happening in the new-issue market.
- *Peter Dickinson's Retirement Letter*, 7811 Montrose Rd., Potomac, MD 20854, 800/777-5005. $49, 12 issues. The best newsletter available for those approaching or in retirement.
- *Richard C. Young's Intelligence Report*, 7811 Montrose Rd., Potomac, MD 20854, 800/777-5005. $177 per year, 12 issues. Advice on stocks, bonds, closed-end funds, no-load funds and other investments, from one of my colleagues at Phillips Publishing.
- *Richard E. Band's Profitable Investing*, 7811 Montrose Rd., Potomac, MD 20854, 800/777-5005. $149 per year, 12 issues. Investment advisor Band's outstanding newsletter on the investment markets.
- *Richard Russell's Dow Theory Letter*, P.O. Box 1759, La Jolla, CA 92038. $225 per year, 26 issues. Edited by one of the all-time greats of Wall Street, this letter offers the next best thing to a free sample—a three-issue trial subscription for $1. I read Dick's letter religiously.

- *The Ruff Times*, P.O. Box 25, Pleasanton, CA 94566, 800/877-7833 or 415/463-2200. $149 per year, 26 issues. Edited by maverick investment guru Howard Ruff, this newsletter is full of interesting adventures.

$ COST-CUTTING TIP #110
Low-Cost Advice from 900 Numbers

Some services offer 900 numbers that give advice on various investment markets. Through these, you can hear opinions and investment recommendations from such top-rated analysts as Bob Kinsman, Bert Dohmen and John Dessauer. The costs range from $1 to $2 per minute.

This may sound like a lot of money—and, true, those 900-number charges can add up. However, calling the hotlines can still be cheaper than subscribing to newsletters or getting personal advice. You can, for example, get the latest recommendations from Michael Murphy, editor of the *Overpriced Stock Service*, a newsletter that normally sells for $995 a year, simply by dialing a 900 number and spending a few dollars. Or, you can get the latest advice from Bert Dohmen, who charges $1,800 an hour for personal consultations, by calling the 900 service that carries his advice. The $2 per minute charge you pay adds up to only $120 an hour—far less than his normal hourly fee. (But his commentary only lasts a few minutes.)

Here's a selection of 900 numbers you can call for financial advice:

- 1/900/234-7777: Offers advice from over a dozen services around the country, including Bert Dohmen's *Wellington Letter* and Stan Weinstein's *Professional Tape Reader*. $2 per minute.
- 1/900/468-7833: Advice from best-selling investment author Howard Ruff. $2 for the first minute, $1 for each additional minute.
- 1/900/446-1111: Operated by the discount brokerage firm Quick & Reilly, this line offers the latest advice from 15 independent newsletter advisors including Michael Murphy of the highly rated

California Technology Stock Letter and John Dessauer, a regular panelist on "Wall Street Week" and the editor of *Dessauer's Journal of Financial Markets*.

- 1/900/963-9963: Offers two dozen up-to-date messages from various advisors. $1.75 for the first minute; $1.00 for each additional minute.
- 1/900/990-0909: Taped messages from advisors ranging from the staid "Wall Street Week" panelist Frank Cappiello to the defiantly antiestablishment Larry Abraham (press 150# on your touch-tone phone).

$ COST-CUTTING TIP #111
Get a Free Sample of Mark Skousen's Newsletter

Last, but not least, I've arranged with my publisher, Phillips Publishing, for all readers of this book to receive a free sample of my newsletter, *Forecasts & Strategies*. My letter comes out monthly, with an additional three to four special reports and alerts a year. You can also subscribe at the specially reduced rate of $99 for the first year (regularly, $177 per year). Included in my monthly letter are regular features on outlook for the economy, new ways to invest, speculator's corner, taxes, privacy corner and Scrooge investing techniques. Order your first issue today by contacting Phillips Publishing, 7811 Montrose Rd., Potomac, MD 20854, 800/777-5005 or 301/340-2100.

CHAPTER 17

Conclusion: The Philosophy of the Scrooge Investor

Most of the great investors are misers.

—WARREN BUFFETT

IN THE previous 16 chapters, we have applied the Scrooge philosophy to a wide variety of investments—stocks, bonds, mutual funds, real estate, precious metals and foreign investments. But, in a very real sense, the Scrooge philosophy should encompass all your financial activities.

What is this Scrooge philosophy?

- Scrooge investors are productive citizens, always seeking opportunities to make money by offering goods or services that people can really use.
- Scrooge investors look for new trends and opportunities ahead of the crowd.
- Scrooge investors keep track of their expenses, even down to the last penny.
- Scrooge investors always live within their means, avoiding wasteful consumer expenditures.
- Scrooge investors avoid consumer debt like the plague, paying in cash whenever possible.
- Scrooge investors borrow money for business purposes only when

absolutely essential and then make sure their earnings always exceed their interest expenses.

• Scrooge investors are always cost conscious in business, investments and their personal affairs.

• Scrooge investors build their net worth no matter how much they spend each month.

• Scrooge investors develop a consistent savings program.

• Scrooge investors take advantage of the knowledge and wisdom of the best experts in other fields.

• Scrooge investors stay in good physical and mental shape, knowing that "if you're not healthy, you're not wealthy."

Famous Scrooge Investors

There are many examples of wealthy individuals who have followed this advice. I've referred already to fictional characters who have followed the Scrooge philosophy. What about contemporary examples?

John D. Rockefeller, Jr., the oil magnate who became America's first billionaire, was always cost conscious. He always had a goal of achieving something big. To achieve it, he worked hard and looked for exciting new opportunities. Discipline, order and thrift were habits he formed early in life. He kept a financial journal, *Ledger A*, in which he wrote down, day by day and to the penny, his income, expenses, savings, investments and business affairs. He was careful not to spend too much on clothing and other consumer goods. In short, he was destined for financial independence.

J. Paul Getty, another oil billionaire, had extensive experience in all areas of business and investing. He was a high-flying speculator, but always practiced economy and discipline and used others' expertise. "Make your money first—then think about spending it," he advised. He was a hard worker. "I still find it's often necessary to work 16 to 18 hours a day, and sometimes around the clock." Getty was an inveterate bargain hunter. In the stock market, he bought stocks during the 1930s depression when everyone else was scared. "Get-rich-quick schemes just don't work," he said. He recommended buying low-priced stocks in "industries that cannot help but burgeon as time goes on."

John Templeton, who runs one of the most successful mutual funds in the 20th century, is a strong believer in the Scrooge philosophy. During the 1930s depression, he saved 50% of his income! He avoids consumer debt—in fact, he bought his first home with cash. He works hard, putting in 60 hours a week. In selecting stocks, he looks for companies around the world that offer low prices and an excellent long-term outlook. "If you're going to buy the best bargains, look in more than one industry, and look in more than one nation." He adds, "Avoid investing in those countries with a high level of socialism or government regulation of business."

Warren Buffett, the Omaha billionaire, takes a strong business approach to investing. He also works long hours. He learned frugality from his father, a congressman who strongly opposed government waste. Buffett concentrates on only a few companies and gets to know them well. He avoids poorly managed companies, no matter how enticing the bargain price. "We try to buy not only good businesses, but ones run by high-grade, talented and likeable managers." According to Buffett, good managers are dedicated cost-cutters who know the budget of everything in their company. Just as cost-conscious businesses are the most profitable, so cost-conscious investors are all the more successful. He searches for stocks that can be bought for less than they're worth. When buying a company, Buffett takes a conservative approach. Instead of buying common stocks, for example, he tends to buy preferred convertible stock, which earns income, limits his downside risk and offers upside potential.

Stingy or Just Careful?

The greatest temptation facing every Scrooge investor is to be too much of a skinflint, unwilling to let go of any money that comes his or her way. Before his repentance and change of heart, Ebenezer Scrooge adamantly refused to give anything to charity. "Bah, humbug!" he responded. "I wish to be left alone." Yet it is clear that Charles Dickens's famous character was not a happy man. Every Scrooge investor must discover, as did the original Scrooge, that happiness is achieved by living life to the fullest, for him- or herself and everyone that he or she meets. This change in attitude also means expressing gratitude to the free-enterprise system and a nation that gives one the chance to be financially successful. For without freedom, a sound legal system and a stable political environment, only a few prosper. Most business people and investors suffer. Just as the shrewd gambler always leaves something on the table, so the wise investor should return some money to the system through charitable giving or donations to foundations dedicated to free enterprise.

Arkad, the main character in *The Richest Man in Babylon*, expresses the true spirit of financial stewardship when he states, "A part of all you earn is yours to keep." Note that he said "a part"—not all. George Clason, the author of this classic, the greatest financial book ever written, describes Arkad's approach as follows: "In old Babylon there once lived a certain very rich man named Arkad. Far and wide he was famed for his great wealth. Also was he famed for his liberality. He was generous with his family. He was liberal in his own expenses. But nevertheless each year his wealth increased more rapidly than he spent it."

It is possible and even prudent to follow Arkad's lead in *The Richest Man in Babylon*. You can be generous in your expenditures and still become richer every year. It's not how much you earn, or even how much you spend, that really matters. It's how much you keep. And if you are going to keep anything, you must follow the Scrooge philosophy in everything you do:

ALWAYS SPEND LESS THAN YOU EARN!

Index

About the Author

MARK SKOUSEN has been a lifelong practitioner of Scrooge investing. He has always believed in thrift, hard work, staying out of debt and taking advantage of bargains. He started with very little and paid his way through college. When he graduated with honors, he had a fully-paid-for new car, a full-time job and money in his pocket—plus a fiancée who has been the secret to his success!

Today, Mark Skousen is financially independent and spends his time writing and researching on investment and economic topics. He is the author of 14 books, including *High Finance on a Low Budget* (coauthored with his wife, Jo Ann), *The Complete Guide to Financial Privacy* and *Economics on Trial*. He received his Ph.D. in economics from George Washington University. He is currently Adjunct Professor of Economics and Finance at Rollins College in Winter Park, Florida. Students often recognize him driving around campus in his restored 1958 MGA automobile.

Professor Skousen also writes a monthly investment newsletter, *Forecasts & Strategies*, one of the largest investment letters in the country. In his spare time, he enjoys basketball, softball, collecting old books and reading *Uncle Scrooge* comic books to his five children.